## 365
# ONE-MINUTE MEDITATIONS

# GOD CALLING

### FROM THE LIFE-CHANGING
### DEVOTIONAL CLASSIC

365
ONE-MINUTE MEDITATIONS

# GOD CALLING

FROM THE LIFE-CHANGING
DEVOTIONAL CLASSIC

BARBOUR
PUBLISHING

*God Calling* © John Hunt Publishing, Ltd., New Alresford, Hants, UK

*365 One-Minute Meditations from God Calling* © 2008 John Hunt Publishing, Ltd.

Editorial assistance by Jill Jones.

ISBN 978-1-60260-052-2

Published by Barbour Publishing, Inc., P.O. Box 719, Uhrichsville, Ohio 44683, www.barbourbooks.com

*Our mission is to publish and distribute inspirational products offering exceptional value and biblical encouragement to the masses.*

Printed in China.

# A MINUTE A DAY CAN CHANGE YOUR LIFE.

We're all busy and pressed for time. But somewhere in our daily schedule, there must be at least sixty free seconds. Look for that open minute and fill it with this book. *365 One-Minute Meditations from God Calling* provides a quick but powerful reading for every day of the year, promising real spiritual impact. Each day's entry features a carefully selected verse from God's Word, along with a condensed reading from *God Calling*, one of the most beloved devotionals of all time.

First published some seventy-five years ago, *God Calling* is still changing lives with its inspiring message of God's love and care for His people. These excerpts are taken from the classic edition of the book, with only the lightest editing for clarity.

If you're seeking a spiritual lift, try *365 One-Minute Meditations from God Calling*. You'll only need a moment per day—but the benefits could be life-changing.

# BETWEEN THE YEARS

*I am the light of the world: he that followeth me shall not walk in darkness, but shall have the light of life.*

JOHN 8:12

I stand between the years. The light of My presence is flung across the year to come—the radiance of the Sun of righteousness.

Dwell not on the past—only on the present. Only use the past as the trees use My sunlight to absorb it, to make from it in after days the warming fire-rays. So store only the blessings from Me, the Light of the world.

# ARM OF LOVE

*Be of good courage, and he shall strengthen thine heart:*

*wait, I say, on the LORD.*

PSALM 27:14

You are to help to save others. Never let one day pass when you have not reached out an arm of love to someone outside your home.

Each day do something to lift another soul out of the sea of sin or disease or doubt into which man has fallen.

The helping hand is needed that raises the helpless to courage, to struggle, to faith, to health.

# THE WAY WILL OPEN

*They that wait upon the L*ORD *shall renew their strength.*

ISAIAH 40:31

You must be renewed, remade. Christ, Christ, Christ. Everything must rest on Me. Only love is a conquering force. Be not afraid; I will help you.

Take heart. God loves, God helps, God fights, God wins. You shall see. You shall know. The way will open. All My love has ever planned, all My love has ever thought, you shall see each day unfold. Only be taught. Just be a child. A child never questions plans. A child accepts gladly.

# DO NOT PLAN

*Come unto me, all ye that labour and are heavy laden,*

*and I will give you rest.*

MATTHEW 11:28

All is well. Wonderful things are happening. Do not limit God at all. He cares and provides.

Uproot self—the channel blocker. Do not plan ahead; the way will unfold step by step. Leave tomorrow's burden. Christ is the great burden bearer. You cannot bear His load, and He only expects you to carry a little day-share.

# HOARD NOTHING

*Commit thy way unto the Lord; trust also in him;*

*and he shall bring it to pass.*

**PSALM 37:5**

Love Me and do My will. No evil shall befall you. Take no thought for tomorrow. Rest in My presence brings peace. Do not be afraid of poverty. Let money flow freely. I will let it flow in, but you must let it flow out. I never send money to stagnate—only to those who pass it on. Keep nothing for yourself. Hoard nothing. Only have what you need and use. This is My law of discipleship.

# SHARP AND READY

*Study to shew thyself approved unto God, a workman that needeth not to be ashamed, rightly dividing the word of truth.*

## 2 TIMOTHY 2:15

Never neglect these times; pray and read your Bible and train and discipline yourself. That is your work—Mine is to use you. But My instruments must be sharp and ready. Then I use them.

Discipline and perfect yourself at all costs. Do this, for soon every fleeting thought will be answered, every wish gratified, every deed used. Oh! Be careful that you ask nothing amiss—nothing that is not according to My Spirit.

# THE SECRET PEARL

*A word fitly spoken is like apples of gold in pictures of silver.*

**PROVERBS 25:11**

Each word or thought of yours can be like a pearl that you drop into the secret place of another heart, and in some hour of need, lo! the recipient finds the treasure and realizes for the first time its value.

Do not be too ready to do; just be. I said, "Be ye therefore perfect," not "do" perfect things. Try to grasp this. Individual efforts avail nothing. It is only the work of My Spirit that counts.

# LOVE BANGS THE DOOR

*They that trust in the LORD shall be as mount Zion,*

*which cannot be removed, but abideth for ever.*

**PSALM 125:1**

Life with Me is not immunity from difficulties, but peace in difficulties. My guidance is often by shut doors. Love bangs as well as opens.

Joy is the result of faithful, trusting acceptance of My will. Saint Paul, My servant, learned this lesson of the banged doors when he said, "Our light affliction, which is but for a moment, worketh for us a far more exceeding and eternal weight of glory."

# No Strain

*Rest in the Lord, and wait patiently for him.*

**Psalm 37:7**

Rest in Me. Do not feel the strain of life. Do you not see I am a master instrument maker? Have I not fashioned each part? Do I not know just what it can bear without a strain? Would I, the maker of so delicate an instrument, ask of it anything that could destroy or strain?

No! The strain is only when you are serving another master, the world, fame, the good opinion of men—or carrying two days' burden on the one day.

# INFLUENCE

*For God so loved the world, that he gave his only begotten Son, that whosoever believeth in him should not perish, but have everlasting life.*

JOHN 3:16

When you come to Me, and I give you that eternal life I give to all who believe in Me, it alters your whole existence, the words you speak, the influences you have.

These are all eternal. They spring from the life within you, My life, so that they, too, live forever. Now you see how vast, how stupendous, is the work of any soul who has eternal life.

# THE ACHE OF LOVE

*The sheep follow him: for they know his voice.*

JOHN 10:4

"I am the light of the world," but sometimes in tender pity I withhold too glaring a light, lest, in its dazzling brightness, you should miss your daily path and work.

At the moment you are pilgrims and need only your daily marching orders and strength and guidance for the day. The trust given to Me today takes away the ache of the rejection of My love that I suffered on earth and have suffered through the ages.

# THANKS FOR TRIALS

*In every thing give thanks: for this is the will of God*

*in Christ Jesus concerning you.*

**1 THESSALONIANS 5:18**

You must say "thank You" for everything, even seeming trials and worries.

Joy is the whole being's attitude of "thank You" to Me. Be glad. Rejoice. A father loves to see his children happy. Seek to find a heart-home for each truth I have imparted to you. Use all I give you. Help others. I ache to find a way into each life and heart.

# FRIENDS UNSEEN

*Casting all your care upon him; for he careth for you.*

1 PETER 5:7

Your lives shall not be all care. Gold does not stay in the crucible—only until it is refined. Already I hear the music and the marching of the unseen host, rejoicing at your victory.

No follower of Mine would ever err or fall if once the veil were withdrawn that prevents him seeing how these slips disappoint those who long for him to conquer in My strength and name, and the ecstasy of rejoicing when victory is won.

# MIGHTY AND MARVELOUS

*I protest by your rejoicing which I have in Christ Jesus our Lord, I die daily.*

### 1 CORINTHIANS 15:31

Glad indeed are the souls with whom I walk. The coming of My Spirit into a life, and its working, is imperceptible, but the result is mighty.

When I bore your sins in My own body on the tree, I bore the self-human nature of the world. As you, too, kill self, you gain the overwhelming power I released for a weary world.

# Relax

*Jesus came and spake unto them, saying,*

*All power is given unto me in heaven and in earth.*

MATTHEW 28:18

Relax, do not get tense, have no fear. All is for the best.

How can you fear change when your life is hid with Me in

God, who changes not?

Claim My power. The same power with which I cast out

devils is yours today.

You cannot ask too much. Never think you are too busy.

As long as you get back to Me and replenish after each task,

no work can be too much.

# FRIEND IN DRUDGERY

*Behold, I am the LORD, the God of all flesh:*

*is there any thing too hard for me?*

JEREMIAH 32:27

It is the daily strivings that count, not the momentary heights. The obeying of My will day in, day out, in the wilderness plains, rather than the occasional Mount of Transfiguration.

Perseverance is nowhere needed so much as in the religious life. The drudgery of the kingdom it is that secures My intimate friendship. I am the Lord of little things. Nothing in the day is too small to be a part of My scheme.

# GOD'S RUSH TO GIVE

*Trust in the LORD with all thine heart; and lean not unto thine own*

*understanding. In all thy ways acknowledge him,*

*and he shall direct thy paths.*

PROVERBS 3:5–6

Abide in My love. This is your part to carry out, and then I surround you with a protective screen that keeps all evil from you. It is fashioned by your own attitude of mind, words, and deeds.

I want to give you all things, good measure, pressed down, and running over. You know little yet of the divine impatience that longs to rush to give.

# FAITH-WORKS

*Behold, his soul which is lifted up is not upright in him:*

*but the just shall live by his faith.*

## HABAKKUK 2:4

Pray daily for faith. It is My gift.

It is your only requisite for the accomplishment of mighty deeds. Certainly you have to work, you have to pray, but upon faith alone depends the answer to your prayers— your works.

I give it you in response to your prayer. And yet "faith without works is dead." So you need works, too, to feed your faith in Me.

# LOVE ANTICIPATES

*Now unto him that is able to do exceeding abundantly above all that we ask*

*or think, according to the power that worketh in us. . .*

EPHESIANS 3:20

None ever sought Me in vain. I wait with a hungry longing
to be called upon; and I, who have seen your heart's needs
before you cried upon Me, am already preparing the answer.
The anticipatory love of God is a thing mortals seldom
realize. Dismiss the thought of a grudging God who had
to be petitioned with tears and much speaking before
reluctantly He loosed the desired treasures.

# AT ONE WITH GOD

*For as he thinketh in his heart, so is he.*

### PROVERBS 23:7

One with Me. One with the Lord of the whole universe!

If you realize your high privilege, you have only to think and immediately the object of your thought is called into being. "Set your affection on things above, not on things on the earth."

To dwell in thought on the material, when once you live in Me, is to call it into being. So you must be careful only to think of and desire that which will help your spiritual growth.

# A CROWDED DAY

*So that we may boldly say, The Lord is my helper,*

*and I will not fear what man shall do unto me.*

HEBREWS 13:6

Believe that I am with you and controlling all. When My Word has gone forth, all are powerless against it.

You have much to learn. Go on until you can take the most crowded day with a song. The finest accompaniment to a song of praise to Me is a very crowded day. Let love be the motif running through all.

Do not get worried. I am your helper. "Underneath are the everlasting arms."

# Gray Days

*Fear thou not; for I am with thee: be not dismayed; for I am thy God:*
*I will strengthen thee; yea, I will help thee; yea, I will uphold thee with*
*the right hand of my righteousness.*

ISAIAH 41:10

Never forget your "thank You." Do you not see it is a lesson?
You must say "thank You" on the grayest days. All cannot be
light unless you do.

If a gray day is not one of thankfulness, the lesson has
to be repeated until it is. A great work requires a great and
careful training.

# How Power Comes

*When thou prayest, enter into thy closet, and when thou hast shut thy*

*door, pray to thy Father which is in secret; and thy Father*

*which seeth in secret shall reward thee openly.*

MATTHEW 6:6

All power is given unto Me. It is Mine to give, Mine to withhold, but even I have to acknowledge that I cannot withhold it from the soul who dwells near Me.

It is breathed in by the soul who lives in My presence. Learn to shut yourself away in My presence—and then, without speaking, you have those things you desire of Me— strength, power, joy, riches.

# YOUR GREAT REWARD

*He that abideth in me, and I in him,*

*the same bringeth forth much fruit: for without me ye can do nothing.*

JOHN 15:5

You pray for faith, and you are told to do so. But I make provision in the house of My abiding for those who turn toward Me and yet have weak knees and hearts that faint. I am your guide. I very rarely grant the long vista to My disciples, especially in personal affairs, for one step at a time is the best way to cultivate faith.

# The Way of Happiness

*I beseech you therefore, brethren, by the mercies of God, that ye present*

*your bodies a living sacrifice, holy, acceptable unto God,*

*which is your reasonable service.*

Romans 12:1

Complete surrender of every moment to God is the

foundation of happiness; the superstructure is the joy of

communion with Him. That is the mansion I went to

prepare for you.

My followers have misunderstood that and looked too

often upon that promise as referring only to an afterlife, and

too often upon this life as something to be struggled through

to get the reward of the next.

# Keep Calm

*Keep thy heart with all diligence; for out of it are the issues of life.*

PROVERBS 4:23

Keep your spirit-life calm and unruffled. Nothing else matters. Leave all to Me. This is your great task, to get calm in My presence, not to let one ruffled feeling stay for one moment. Years of blessing may be checked in one moment by that.

No matter who frets you or what, yours is the task to stop all else until absolute calm comes. Any block means My power diverted into other channels.

# HEIGHT OF THE STORM

*Shew me thy ways, O Lord; teach me thy paths.*

PSALM 25:4

Fear not. It is to the drowning man the rescuer comes. To the brave swimmer who can fare well alone, He comes not.

It is a part of My method to wait till the storm is at its full violence. So did I with My disciples on the lake. I could have bidden the first angry wave be calm, but what a lesson unlearned.

My disciples thought that in sleep I had forgotten them. Remember how mistaken they were.

# LOW AMBITIONS

*Therefore will the LORD wait, that he may be gracious unto you.*

ISAIAH 30:18

How best can you serve? Let that be your daily seeking, not how best you can be served.

Do the aims and ambitions that man strives for bring peace, or the world's awards bring heart-rest and happiness? No! Those whom the world has most rewarded, with name, fame, honor, wealth, are weary and disappointed.

And yet to the listening ear, there echoes My message "Come unto Me, all ye that are weary and heavy laden, and I will give you rest."

# I Clear the Path

*The steps of a good man are ordered by the Lord.*

PSALM 37:23

I can see the future. I know better than you what you need. Trust Me absolutely. You are not at the mercy of fate or buffeted about by others. You are being led in a very definite way, and others, who do not serve your purpose, are being moved out of your path.

Trust me for all. Your very extremity will ensure My activity for you. Literally, you have to depend on Me for everything.

# THE SOUL AT WAR

*There hath no temptation taken you but such as is common to man: but God is faithful, who will not suffer you to be tempted above that ye are able.*

### 1 CORINTHIANS 10:13

Love, joy, peace—welcome these. Singly, they are miracle-producing, but together they can command all that is needed on the physical, mental, and spiritual planes.

You have to see your inner lives are all they should be, and then the work is accomplished. Not in rushing and striving on the material plane, but on the battlefield of the soul are these things won.

# SUFFERING REDEEMS

*For I know the thoughts that I think toward you, saith the LORD,*

*thoughts of peace, and not of evil, to give you an expected end.*

**JEREMIAH 29:11**

All sacrifice and all suffering are redemptive: to teach the individual or to be used to raise and help others.

Nothing is by chance.

The divine mind, and its wonder working, is beyond your finite mind to understand.

No detail is forgotten in My plans, already perfect.

# ANOTHER START

*It is of the LORD's mercies that we are not consumed, because his compassions fail not. They are new every morning: great is thy faithfulness.*

### LAMENTATIONS 3:22–23

Take courage. Start a new life tomorrow. Put the old mistakes away. I give you a fresh start. If My forgiveness were for the righteous only, where would be its need?

Remember, "To whom much is forgiven, the same loveth much."

Why do you fret and worry so? I wait to give you all that is lovely, but your lives are soiled with worry and fret. I can only bless glad, thankful hearts.

# PRACTICE LOVE

*This is his commandment. . .love one another, as he gave us commandment.*

### 1 JOHN 3:23

Want of love will block the way. You must love all, those who fret you and those who do not.

Practice love. It is a great lesson, and you have a great Teacher. You must love; how otherwise can you dwell in Me, where nothing unloving can come? Practice this, and I will bless you exceedingly, above all you can not only ask, but imagine.

# IF MEN OPPOSE

*Be not afraid, only believe.*

**MARK 5:36**

Only believe. Was it axes or human implements that brought the walls of Jericho down? Rather the songs of praise of the people and My thought carried out in action.

All walls shall fall before you, too. There is no earth-power. It falls like a house of paper at My miracle-working touch. Your faith and My power—the only two essentials.

So if man's petty opposition still holds good, it is only because I choose to let it stand between you and what would be a mistake for you.

# DROP YOUR CRUTCH

*God hath spoken once; twice have I heard this;*

*that power belongeth unto God.*

PSALM 62:11

Just go step by step. My will shall be revealed as you go. You will never cease to be thankful for this time when you felt at peace and trustful, and yet had no human security.

When human support or material help is removed, My power can become operative. I cannot teach a man to walk who is trusting a crutch. Away with your crutch, and My power shall so invigorate you that you shall indeed walk on to victory.

# YOU SHALL KNOW

*If any man will do his will, he shall know of the doctrine,*
*whether it be of God, or whether I speak of myself.*

JOHN 7:17

Walk with Me. I will teach you. Listen to Me. I will speak.
As you persist and make a life-habit of this, in many
marvelous ways I will reveal My will to you. You shall have
more sure knowing of both the present and the future.
Life is a school. Believe that your problems and difficulties
can be explained by Me more clearly than by any other.

# God's Longing

*I wait for the Lord, my soul doth wait, and in his word do I hope.*

PSALM 130:5

Think of the multitudes who thronged Me when I was on earth, all eager for something. Think as I supplied their many wants and granted their manifold requests, what it meant to Me to find amid the crowd some one or two who followed Me just to be near Me, just to dwell in My presence.

Comfort Me awhile by letting Me know that you would seek Me just to dwell in My presence.

# LIGHT AHEAD

*Before they call, I will answer; and while they are yet speaking, I will hear.*

### ISAIAH 65:24

Only a few steps more and then My power shall be seen and known. You are now walking in the tunnel-darkness. Soon you shall be a light to guide feet that are afraid.

The cries of your sufferings have pierced even to the ears of God Himself. To hear, with God, is to answer. For only a cry from the heart, a cry to divine power to help human weakness, ever reaches the ear divine.

# ON ME ALONE

*Let patience have her perfect work, that ye may be perfect and entire,*
*wanting nothing.*

### JAMES 1:4

I am your Lord, your supply. You must rely on Me. Trust to the last uttermost limit. You must depend on divine power only. I have not forgotten you. Your help is coming. You shall know and realize My power.

Endurance is faith tried almost to the breaking point. You must wait and trust and hope and joy in Me. You must not depend on man but on Me—on Me, your strength, your help, your supply.

# THE VOICE DIVINE

*Be still, and know that I am God.*

PSALM 46:10

The divine voice is not always expressed in words. It is made known as a heart-consciousness.

# THE LIFELINE

*From the end of the earth will I cry unto thee, when my heart is overwhelmed: lead me to the rock that is higher than I.*

PSALM 61:2

Look to Me for salvation. Did not My servant of old say, "All Thy waves and Thy billows are gone over me"? But not all the waters of affliction could drown him. For of him was it true, "He came from above, He took me, He drew me out of many waters."

The lifeline is the line from the soul to God, faith, and power.

# THE DIFFICULT PATH

*Wait on the LORD, and keep his way.*

PSALM 37:34

Your path is difficult. There is no work in life so hard as waiting, and yet I say wait. Wait until I show you My will. Proof it is of My love and of My certainty of your true discipleship that I give you hard tasks.

Again, I say, wait. All motion is easier than calm waiting. So many of My followers have marred their work and hindered the progress of My kingdom by activity. Wait. I will not overtry your spiritual strength.

# MEET ME EVERYWHERE

*For as many as are led by the Spirit of God, they are the sons of God.*

## ROMANS 8:14

Life is really consciousness of Me.

Have no fear. A very beautiful future lies before you. Let it be a new life, a new existence, in which in every single happening, event, plan, you are conscious of Me.

Get this ever-consciousness and you have eternal life. Be in all things led by the Spirit of God and trust Me in all. And the consciousness of Me must bring joy. Give Me not only trust but gladness.

# NEAR THE GOAL

*Let us not be weary in well doing: for in due season we shall reap,*
*if we faint not.*

## GALATIANS 6:9

In a race it is not the start that hurts. It is when the goal is in sight that heart and nerves and courage and muscles are strained almost beyond human endurance.

In the annals of heaven, the saddest records are those that tell of the many who ran well until in sight of the goal, and then their courage failed. The whole host of heaven longed to cry out how near the end was, but they fell out, never to know until the last day of revealing how near they were to victory.

# In My Presence

*Blessed is the man that heareth me, watching daily at my gates,*

*waiting at the posts of my doors.*

PROVERBS 8:34

You do not realize that you would have broken down under the weight of your cares but for the renewing time with Me. It is not what I say; it is I Myself. It is not the hearing Me so much as the being in My presence.

Gradually you will be transformed, physically, mentally, spiritually, into My likeness. All who see you or have contact with you will be brought near to Me.

# INSPIRATION—NOT ASPIRATION

*There is a spirit in man: and the inspiration of the Almighty*
*giveth them understanding.*

JOB 32:8

The world does not need supermen, but supernatural men.
Men who will persistently turn the self out of their lives and
let divine power work through them.

Let inspiration take the place of aspiration. I have always
plenty of work to be done and always pay My workpeople
well, as you will see, as more and more you get the right
attitude of thought about the work being Mine only.

# NEVER RUFFLED

*Thou wilt keep him in perfect peace, whose mind is stayed on thee:*

*because he trusteth in thee.*

ISAIAH 26:3

Be still, be calm. Wait before Me. Learn of Me patience, humility, peace. When will you be absolutely unruffled whatever happens? You are slow to learn your lesson. In the rush and work and worry, the very seeking a silence must help.

In bustle so little is accomplished. You must learn to take the calm with you in the most hurried days.

# PSYCHIC POWERS

*It is good for me to draw near to God.*

PSALM 73:28

Psychic powers are not necessarily spiritual powers. Do not seek the spiritual through material means. Could you but see, it is weighing beautiful spirit-wings down with earth's mud. Seek this time as a time of communion with Me—not as a time to ask questions and have them answered.

Do not expect a perfect church, but find in a church the means of coming very near to Me. That alone matters.

# LET ME DO IT

*Mary. . .sat at Jesus' feet, and heard his word. . . . Mary hath chosen
that good part, which shall not be taken away from her.*

## LUKE 10:39, 42

It is not passionate appeal that gains the divine ear so much
as the quiet placing of the difficulty in the divine hands. So
trust as a child who places his tangled skein of wool in the
hands of a loving mother and runs out to play, pleasing the
mother more by his unquestioning confidence than if he
went down on his knees and implored her help.

# ENDURE

*I will give thee the treasures of darkness, and hidden riches of secret places,*

*that thou mayest know that I, the LORD, which call thee by thy name,*

*am the God of Israel.*

ISAIAH 45:3

Meet all your difficulties with love and laughter. I am with you. Do not fail Me. I cannot fail you.

How many of the world's prayers have gone unanswered because My children who prayed did not endure to the end. They thought it was too late, that I was not going to act for them. "He that endureth to the end shall be saved."

# CLAIM YOUR RIGHTS

*Give us this day our daily bread.*

MATTHEW 6:11

"In every thing by prayer and supplication let your requests be made known unto God."

But do not beg. Rather come as a business manager bringing to the owner the needs, checks to be signed, and so on, and knowing that to lay the matter before him means immediate supply.

I long to supply, but the asking is necessary, because to you that contact with Me is vital.

# NOTHING CAN HURT

*Who shall separate us from the love of Christ?*

ROMANS 8:35

Only self can cast a shadow on the way. Be more afraid of spirit-unrest, of soul-disturbance, than of earthquake or fire. When you feel the absolute calm has been broken—away alone with Me until your heart sings and all is strong and calm.

All that you have to do is to keep calm and happy. God does the rest. No evil force can hinder My power—only you have power to do that.

# You Must Trust

*He shall cover thee with his feathers, and under his wings shalt thou trust.*

PSALM 91:4

You must trust Me wholly. This lesson has to be learned. You shall be helped; you shall be guided continually. The children of Israel would long before have entered the Promised Land—only their doubts and fears continually drove them back into the wilderness. Are you trusting all to Me or not? All your doubts arrest My work. I died to save you from sin and doubt and worry. You must believe in Me absolutely.

# SECRET OF HEALING

*But unto you that fear my name shall the Sun of righteousness*

*arise with healing in his wings.*

**MALACHI 4:2**

Love the busy life. It is a joy-filled life. I love you and bid you be of good cheer.

Live outside whenever possible. Sun and air are My great healing forces.

Never forget that real healing of body, mind, and spirit comes from within, from the close, loving contact of your spirit with My Spirit.

# Share Everything

*All things are of God, who hath reconciled us to himself by Jesus Christ,*
*and hath given to us the ministry of reconciliation.*

2 Corinthians 5:18

Share your love, your joy, your happiness, your time, your food, gladly with all. Such wonders will unfold. You see it all but in bud now—the glory of the open flower is beyond all your telling. Give out love and all you can with a glad, free heart and hand. Use all you can for others, and back will come such countless stores and blessings.

# HOW TO CONQUER

*Nay, in all these things we are more than conquerors*
*through him that loved us.*

ROMANS 8:37

Set your standard high. Aim at conquering a world all around you. Just say, "Jesus conquers"—"Jesus saves"—in the face of every doubt, sin, evil, fear.

No evil can stand against that, for "there is none other name under heaven given among men, whereby men can be saved." To every thought of want or lack, "Jesus saves from poverty"; to every fear, "Jesus saves from fear."

Do this to every ill and it will vanish.

# SWIFT HELP

*If ye had faith as a grain of mustard seed, ye might say unto this sycamine*

*tree, Be thou plucked up by the root, and be thou planted in the sea;*

*and it should obey you.*

### LUKE 17:6

Pray for more faith, as a thirsty man in a desert prays for
water. Swift and strong comes My help. Do you know what
it is to feel sure that I can never fail you? As sure as you are
that you still breathe? How poor is man's faith! Pray daily and
most diligently that your faith may increase.

# Spirit Sounds

*For she said within herself, If I may but touch his garment, I shall be whole.*

MATTHEW 9:21

Seek sometimes not even to hear Me. Seek a silence of spirit-understanding with Me.

Remember, I "touched her hand, and the fever left her." Not many words, just a moment's contact, and all fever left her. She was well, able to arise and "minister unto them."

My touch is still a potent healer. Sense My presence, and the fever of work and care and fear just melts into nothingness—and health, joy, peace, take its place.

# PERFECT WORK

*In the morning, rising up a great while before day, he went out,*
*and departed into a solitary place, and there prayed.*

MARK 1:35

Times of prayer are times of growth. Cut those times short
and many well-filled hours of work may be profitless.
Heaven's values are so different from the values of earth.
From the point of view of the Great Worker, one poor tool,
working all the time but doing bad work, is of small value
compared with the sharp instrument, used only a short time
but which turns out perfect work.

# DRAW NEAR

*As the Father hath loved me, so have I loved you.*

JOHN 15:9

How little man knows and senses My need! My need of love and companionship.

I came "to draw men unto Me," and sweet it is to feel hearts drawing near in love, not for help as much as for tender comradeship.

Many know the need of man; few know the need of Christ.

# SHOWER LOVE

*The righteous cry, and the LORD heareth.*

## PSALM 34:17

Just carry out My wishes and leave Me to carry out yours. Treat Me as Savior and King, but also with the tender intimacy of one much beloved.

Keep to the rules I have laid down for you, persistently, perseveringly, lovingly, patiently, hopefully, and in faith, and every mountain of difficulty shall be laid low, the rough places of poverty shall be made smooth, and all who know you shall know that I am the Lord.

Shower love.

# Spirit Words

*God is a Spirit: and they that worship him must worship him*

*in spirit and in truth.*

## John 4:24

"The words that I speak unto you, they are spirit, and they are life."

Just as much as the words I spoke to My disciples of old. This is your reward for not seeking spirit-communication through a medium. Those who do it can never know the ecstasy, the wonder, of spirit-communication as you know it.

Life, joy, peace, and healing are yours in very full measure. You will see this as you go on.

# GROW LIKE ME

*We all, with open face beholding as in a glass the glory of the Lord,*

*are changed into the same image from glory to glory,*

*even as by the Spirit of the Lord.*

2 CORINTHIANS 3:18

Look at Me often, and unconsciously you will grow like Me. The nearer you get to Me, the more will you see your unlikeness to Me. Your very deep sense of failure is a sure sign that you are growing nearer to Me.

My strength is made perfect in weakness.

# KEY TO HOLINESS

*If any man will come after me, let him deny himself,*

*and take up his cross daily, and follow me.*

LUKE 9:23

Draw near to Me, My child. Contact with Me is the panacea
for all ills.

Remember that truth is many-sided. Have much tender
love and patience for all who do not see as you do.

The elimination of self is the key to holiness and
happiness and can only be accomplished with My help. Study
My life more. Live in My presence. Worship Me.

# FEAR IS EVIL

*God hath not given us the spirit of fear; but of power, and of love,*
*and of a sound mind.*

## 2 TIMOTHY 1:7

Have no fear. Fear is evil, and "perfect love casts out fear."
There is no room for fear in the heart in which I dwell. Fear
destroys hope. It cannot exist where love is, or where faith is.
Fear is the curse of the world. Man is afraid—afraid of
poverty, afraid of loneliness, afraid of unemployment, afraid
of sickness.

Fight fear as you would a plague.

# LOVE AND LAUGH

*Not by might, nor by power, but by my spirit, saith the LORD of hosts.*

## ZECHARIAH 4:6

Work for Me, with Me, through Me. All work to last must be done in My Spirit. How silently My Spirit works. How gently and gradually souls are led into My kingdom.

Love and laughter form the plow that prepares the ground for the seed. If the ground is hard, seed will not grow there.

Prepare the ground; prepare it as I say.

# SURPRISES

*Let the L*ORD *be magnified, which hath pleasure*

*in the prosperity of his servant.*

PSALM 35:27

Many there are who think that I test and train and bend to My will. I, who bade the disciples take up the cross, loved to prepare a feast for them by the lakeside—a little glad surprise, not a necessity, as the feeding of the multitude may have seemed. I loved to give the wine-gift at the marriage feast.

As you love to plan surprises for those who understand and joy in them, so with Me.

# HEAVEN-LIFE

*The flowers appear on the earth; the time of the singing of birds is come,*
*and the voice of the turtle is heard in our land.*

## SONG OF SOLOMON 2:12

The joy of the spring shall be yours in full measure. Revel in the earth's joy. Do not you think that nature is weary, too, of her long months of travail? There will come back a wonderful joy, if you share in her joy now.

You can truly live a life not of earth—a heaven-life here and now.

# NOTHING IS SMALL

*They had a few small fishes: and he blessed. . . . They took up of the broken*
*meat that was left seven baskets. And they that had eaten*
*were about four thousand.*

MARK 8:7–9

Nothing is small to God. In His sight a sparrow is of greater value than a palace, one kindly word of more importance than a statesman's speech.

It is the life in all that has value, and the quality of the life that determines the value. I came to give eternal life.

# Fruit of Joy

*These things have I spoken unto you, that my joy might remain in you,
and that your joy might be full.*

### John 15:11

See the good in everybody. Love the good in them. See your
unworthiness compared with their worth. Love, laugh, make
the world, your little world, happy.

As the ripples caused by a flung stone stir the surface
of a whole pond, so your joy-making shall spread in ever-
widening circles, beyond all anticipation. Joy in Me. Such joy
is eternal.

Centuries after, it is still bearing joy's precious fruit.

# SEEK BEAUTY

*The heavens declare the glory of God;*

*and the firmament sheweth his handywork.*

PSALM 19:1

Draw beauty from every flower and joy from the song of the birds.

When I wanted to express a beautiful thought, I made a lovely flower.

When I want to express to man what I am—what My Father is—I strive to make a very beautiful character.

Think of yourselves as My expression of attributes, and you will strive in all to be as fit an expression for Me as you can.

# SIMPLICITY

*Seek ye first the kingdom of God, and his righteousness;*
*and all these things shall be added unto you.*

MATTHEW 6:33

Simplicity is the keynote of My kingdom. Choose simple things always.

Love and reverence the humble and the simple.

Have only simple things here. Your standard must never be the world's standard.

# SPIRITUALISM

*This I say then, Walk in the Spirit,*
*and ye shall not fulfil the lust of the flesh.*

## GALATIANS 5:16

Spiritualism is wrong. No man should ever be a medium for any spirit other than Mine.

All you should know, all it is well for you to know of My Spirit-kingdom, I will tell you when and how I see best. The limit is set by your own spiritual development. Follow My injunctions in all things.

# GOD'S TOUCH

*Forget not all his benefits. . .who satisfieth thy mouth with good things;*
*so that thy youth is renewed like the eagle's.*

**PSALM 103:2, 5**

Persevere in all I tell you to do. The persistent carrying out of My commands, My desires, will unfailingly bring you, as far as spiritual, mental, and temporal things are concerned, to that place where you would be.

Man's ecstasy is God's touch on quickened, responsive spirit-nerves.

# YOUR CROSS IS YOU

*The peace of God, which passeth all understanding, shall keep your hearts*

*and minds through Christ Jesus.*

## PHILIPPIANS 4:7

Mine is the cross on which the burdens of the world are laid.

How foolish is any of My disciples who seeks to bear his own

burdens, when there is only one place for them—My cross.

The cross given to each one of you is a cross on which

you can crucify the self that hinders progress and joy and

prevents the flow through your being of My invigorating life

and Spirit.

# REFLECT ME

*In returning and rest shall ye be saved; in quietness*
*and in confidence shall be your strength.*

ISAIAH 30:15

All down the ages, men have been too eager to say what they thought about My truth, and so doing, they have grievously erred. Do not say what you think about Me. My words need none of man's explanation. I can explain to each heart.

Make Me real, and leave Me to do My own work. To lead a soul to Me is one thing; to seek to stay with it to interpret mars the first great act.

# No Greater Joy

*There remaineth therefore a rest to the people of God. For he that is entered into his rest, he also hath ceased from his own works, as God did from his.*

### Hebrews 4:9–10

Withdraw into the calm of communion with Me. Rest in that calm and peace. Life knows no greater joy than you will find in converse and companionship with Me.

You are Mine. When the soul finds its home of rest in Me, then it is that its real life begins.

# YOUR RESOLUTIONS

*Call unto me, and I will answer thee, and shew thee great and mighty things, which thou knowest not.*

#### JEREMIAH 33:3

The difficult way is nearly over, but you have learned in it lessons you could learn in no other way. Wrest from Me, by firm and simple trust and persistent prayer, the treasures of My kingdom.

Such wonderful things are coming to you, joy, peace, assurance, security, health, happiness, laughter.

Claim big things now. Nothing is too big. Satisfy the longing of My heart to give.

# COURAGE

*Some trust in chariots, and some in horses:*
*but we will remember the name of the LORD our God.*

**PSALM 20:7**

I am here. Fear not. Can you really trust Me? I am a God of
power, as well as a man of love, so human, yet so divine.
Just trust. I cannot, and I will not, fail you. All is well.
Courage.

# HELP FROM EVERYWHERE

*I delight to do thy will, O my God.*

PSALM 40:8

Your foolish little activities are valueless in themselves. Seemingly trivial or of seemingly great moment, all deeds are alike if directed by Me. Just cease to function except through Me.

I am your Lord; just obey Me as you would expect a faithful, willing secretary to carry out your directions. Just have no choice but Mine, no will but Mine.

I am dependent on no one agency when I am your supply. Through many channels My help and material flow can come.

# ALL IS WELL

*Who hath saved us, and called us with an holy calling. . .*
*according to his own purpose and grace, which was given us*
*in Christ Jesus before the world began.*

2 TIMOTHY 1:9

Remember My words to My disciples, "This kind goeth not out but by prayer and fasting." Can you tread the way I trod? Can you drink of My cup? Say always, "All is well."

Long though the way may seem, there is not one inch too much. I, your Lord, am not only with you on the journey—I planned, and am planning, the journey.

# A BUD OPENED

*Henceforth I call you not servants; for the servant knoweth not what his lord doeth: but I have called you friends.*

**JOHN 15:15**

You cannot have a need I cannot supply. A flower or one thousand pounds—one is no more difficult than the other. Your need is a spiritual need to carry on My work. All spiritual supply is fashioned from love. The flower and the thousand pounds—both fashioned from love to those who need them.

# Until Your Heart Sings

*He ruleth by his power for ever.*

### Psalm 66:7

I am beside you to bless and help you. Waver not in your prayers. They shall be heard. All power is Mine. Say that to yourself often and steadily.

Say it until your heart sings with the joy of the safety and power it means to you.

Use it as a battle cry—"All power is given unto my Lord," "All power is given unto my friend," "All power is given unto my Savior," and then you pass on to victory.

# KNOW ME

*Grow in grace, and in the knowledge of our Lord and Saviour Jesus Christ.*

2 PETER 3:18

I am here. Seek not to know the future. Mercifully I veil it from you.

Faith is too priceless a possession to be sacrificed in order to purchase knowledge. But faith is based on a knowledge of Me.

So remember that this time is not to learn the future, not to receive revelation of the unseen, but to gain an intimate knowledge of Me that will teach you all things and be the very foundation of your faith.

# WONDERS WILL UNFOLD

*My soul melteth for heaviness: strengthen thou me according unto thy word.*

### PSALM 119:28

Daily, steady persistence. Like the wearing away of a stone by steady drops of water, so will your daily persistence wear away all the difficulties and gain success for you and secure your help for others.

Never falter; go forward so boldly, so unafraid. I am beside you to help and strengthen you.

Wonders have unfolded. More still will unfold, beyond your dreams, beyond your hopes.

# FOLLOW YOUR GUIDE

*I will instruct thee and teach thee in the way which thou shalt go:*

*I will guide thee with mine eye.*

PSALM 32:8

What of a man walking through a glorious glade who fretted because ahead there lay a river he might not be able to cross, when all the time that river was spanned by a bridge? And what if he had a friend who knew the way?

So leave your foolish fears and follow Me, your guide, and refuse to consider the problems of tomorrow. My message to you is to trust and wait.

# GO FORWARD

*I can do all things through Christ which strengtheneth me.*

PHILIPPIANS 4:13

Rest in Me, quiet in My love, strong in My power. Think what it is to possess a power greater than any earthly force. A sway greater, and more far-reaching, than that of any earthly king.

No invention, no electricity, no magnetism, no gold, could achieve one millionth part of all that you can achieve by the power of My Spirit. Just think for one moment all that means.

Go forward. You are only beginning the new life.

# EVIL MOUNTAINS

*Ye see then how that by works a man is justified, and not by faith only.*

**JAMES 2:24**

Faith and obedience will remove mountains, mountains of evil, mountains of difficulty. But they must go hand in hand.

# A Life Apart

*Ye shall seek me, and find me, when ye shall search for me*
*with all your heart.*

### Jeremiah 29:13

I reward your seeking with My presence. Seek Me, love Me, joy in Me. No perils can affright you, no discipline exhaust you. Can you hold on in My strength? I need you more than you need Me. Struggle through this time for My sake.

Are you ready to live a life in the world and yet apart with Me? Going forth from your secret times of communion to rescue and save?

# DELIVERANCE

*The Lord knoweth how to deliver the godly out of temptations.*

2 PETER 2:9

Rest in My love. Joy in the very beauty of holiness. You are Mine. Deliverance is here for you, but thankfulness and joy open the gates.

Try in all things to be very glad, very happy, very thankful. It is not to quiet resignation I give My blessings, but to joyful acceptance and anticipation.

Laughter is the outward expression of joy. That is why I urge upon you love and laughter.

**31**
MARCH

# LOVE'S OFFERING

*The LORD seeth not as man seeth; for man looketh on the outward*

*appearance, but the LORD looketh on the heart.*

### 1 SAMUEL 16:7

I judge not by outward appearances. I judge the heart, and I see in your heart one single desire: to do My will. The simplest offering by a child with the one desire to show you love, is it not more loved by you than the offerings of those who love you not?

So, though you may feel that your work has been spoiled and tarnished, I see it as love's offering.

# SHUT OUT FROM GOD

*These that have turned the world upside down are come hither also.*

## ACTS 17:6

Do you not see that you have not yet learned all? Soon you will have mastered your lesson, and then you will truly be able to do all things through Me and My strength.

Did you not see it with My disciples? Timid, faithless followers, and then, so soon, themselves leaders, healers, conquerors, through Me.

# THE PRICELESS BLESSING

*He that hath my commandments, and keepeth them, he it is that loveth me.*

JOHN 14:21

I am here. Here as truly as I was with My disciples of old. Here to help and bless you. Here to company with you. Do you know, even yet, that this is the priceless blessing of your life? I forgive you, as you have prayed Me to, for all neglects of My commands, but start anew from today.

Study My words and carry them out unflinchingly.

# GREATNESS IS SERVICE

*Rejoice in the Lord always: and again I say, Rejoice.*

## PHILIPPIANS 4:4

My child, I am here, your waiting Lord, ready at your call. I am among you as One who serves, meek and holy, ready to be used and commanded. Remember that is the finest quality of greatness—service. I, who could command a universe—I await the commands of My children. Bring Me into everything.

Always humble, meek, and lowly in heart.

Learn this—no position—just a servant.

# DIVINE EFFICIENCY

*That the trial of your faith, being much more precious than of gold that perisheth, though it be tried with fire, might be found unto praise and honour and glory.*

## 1 PETER 1:7

I am all powerful and all knowing, and I have all your affairs in My hands. Divine efficiency, as well as divine power, is being brought to bear on them.

The kingdom of heaven can only be preached by those who have learned to prize the authority of its kingdom. A many-sided training My apostles need. Not one test too much will I lay on you.

# Heart's Interpreter

*Return unto thy rest, O my soul;*

*for the LORD hath dealt bountifully with thee.*

Psalm 116:7

I am the heart's great interpreter. Even souls who are the nearest together have much in their natures that remain a sealed book to each other, and only as I enter and control their lives do I reveal to each the mysteries of the other. Each soul is so different—I alone understand perfectly the language of each and can interpret between the two.

# EASTER JOY

*Take therefore no thought for the morrow.*

MATTHEW 6:34

Let all go this Eastertide. Loosen your hold on earth, its care, its worries, even its joys. Unclasp your hands, relax, and then the tide of Easter joy will come. Put aside all thought of the future, of the past.

So often man, crying out for some blessing, has yet such tight hold on some earth-treasure that he has no hand to receive Mine, as I hold it out in love. A blessing is yours to take. Sacrifice all to that.

# CALVARY

*I am crucified with Christ: nevertheless I live; yet not I,*
*but Christ liveth in me: and the life which I now live in the flesh*
*I live by the faith of the Son of God.*

## GALATIANS 2:20

From the death of My body on the cross springs that new life that is My gift to every man who will accept it.

Die with Me to self—to the human life—and then you will know the rapturous joy of Easter resurrection.

A risen life so glad and free can be yours.

# Marks of the Kingdom

*Come out from among them, and be ye separate, saith the Lord,*

*and touch not the unclean thing; and I will receive you.*

2 Corinthians 6:17

My children must make a stand. Today in life and work, in love and service, My children must be outstanding.

Be ready to stand aside and let the fashions and customs of the world go by, when My glory and My kingdom are thereby served. Be known by the marks that distinguish those of My kingdom. Be ready to confess Me before men.

# RISEN LIFE

*That I may know him, and the power of his resurrection, and the fellowship of his sufferings, being made conformable unto his death.*

## PHILIPPIANS 3:10

The call comes on this My day for all who love Me to arise from earth-bands from all that hinders the risen life. To arise to beauty, to holiness, to joy, to peace, to work inspired by love and joy, to rise from death to life.

Let nothing hinder your risen life. Of that risen life was it truly said: "I live; yet not I, but Christ liveth in me."

# PRIDE BARS THE WAY

*Whatsoever we ask, we receive of him, because we keep his commandments,*
*and do those things that are pleasing in his sight.*

### 1 John 3:22

The rough stone steps of obedience lead up to the mosaic of joy and love that floor My heaven. Where I am is My home—is heaven.

Heaven may be in a sordid slum or a palace, and I can make My home in the humblest heart. I only dwell with the humble. Pride stands sentinel at the door of the heart to shut out the lowly, humble Christ.

*God Calling*

**11**

APRIL

# HOLD YOUR FORT

*Whosoever he be of you that forsaketh not all that he hath,*

*he cannot be my disciple.*

LUKE 14:33

Remember that My followers are to be a peculiar people, separated from among others. Different ways, a different standard of living, different customs, actuated by different motives. Pray for love.

Never yield one point that you have already won. Discipline, discipline. Love it and rejoice. Mountains can be removed by thought—by desire.

# GOLDEN OPPORTUNITY

*Ask, and it shall be given you; seek, and ye shall find; knock,*
*and it shall be opened unto you.*

### MATTHEW 7:7

Man's need is God's chance to help. Man's need is God's golden opportunity for him of letting his faith find expression. That expression of faith is all that God needs to manifest His power. Faith is the key that unlocks the storehouse of God's resources.

You long for perfection and see your bitter failures. I see faithfulness, and I take your poor faithfulness and crown it with perfection.

# GENTLE WITH ALL

*Let love be without dissimulation.*

ROMANS 12:9

Be gentle with all. Try to see the heart I see, to know the pain and difficulty of the other life that I know. Try, before you interview anyone or speak to anyone, to ask Me to act as interpreter between you two.

Just live in the spirit of prayer. In speaking to Me, you find soul-rest. Simple tasks, faithfully done and persisted in, bring their own reward and are mosaics being laid in the pavement of success.

# EQUALLY YOKED

*Thine ears shall hear a word behind thee, saying, This is the way, walk*
*ye in it, when ye turn to the right hand, and when ye turn to the left.*

### ISAIAH 30:21

People waste so much time in seeking to work out what they
see. I declare to you that in seeing My purpose all is done.

Is not the message of My servant Paul now plain: "Be
ye not unequally yoked together with unbelievers"? My
guidance is intensified immeasurably in power when the two
are one in desire to be with Me.

# NEVER FEEL INADEQUATE

*He said unto me, My grace is sufficient for thee:*
*for my strength is made perfect in weakness.*

## 2 CORINTHIANS 12:9

Never feel inadequate for any task. All work here is accomplished by My Spirit, and that can flow through the humblest and lowliest. Rid yourself of self and all is well. Pray about all, but concentrate on a few things until those are accomplished. Strength for your daily, hourly task is provided. Yours is the fault, the sin, if it is unclaimed, and you fail for lack of it.

# LOVE YOUR SERVANTS

*We have known and believed the love that God hath to us. God is love; and he that dwelleth in love dwelleth in God, and God in him.*

1 JOHN 4:16

Dwell on that thought—God is love. Dwell on My actions on earth. See in them love in operation.

You, too, must put love (God) into action in your lives.

God is love. . .no judging.

God is love. . .no resentment.

God is love. . .all patience.

God is love. . .all power.

God is love. . .all supply.

# THE TWO JOYS

*If ye continue in my word, then are ye my disciples indeed; and ye shall know the truth, and the truth shall make you free.*

## JOHN 8:31–32

Joy is of two kinds. The joy born of love and wonder, and the joy born of love and knowledge, and between the experience of the two joys lie discipline, disappointment, almost disillusion.

But combat these in My strength, persevere in obeying My will, accept My discipline, and the second joy will follow.

# NO DARK DAYS

*Love worketh no ill to his neighbour: therefore love is the fulfilling of the law.*

### ROMANS 13:10

Love is God. Love all, even the beggars. Send no one away without a word of cheer, a feeling that you care. I may have put the impulse to come here into some despairing one's heart. Think if you failed Me!

There would be no dark winter days were love in the hearts of all My children.

# Life Is a Love Story

*He brought me to the banqueting house, and his banner over me was love.*

## Song of Solomon 2:4

You need Me. I need you.

My broken world needs you. Many a troubled heart will be drawn nearer to Me by you.

Oh! It is a glorious way, the upward way, the wonderful discoveries, the tender intimacies, the amazing, almost incomprehensible understanding. Truly the Christian life—life with Me—is a love story.

All you have missed you will find in Me.

You cannot put too great a strain upon My love and forbearance.

# HEART'S AGONY

*We have not an high priest which cannot be touched with the feeling of our infirmities; but was in all points tempted like as we are, yet without sin.*

## HEBREWS 4:15

There is a Calvary-cross on which One hangs alone, untended by even the nearest and dearest.

But beside that cross there stands another, and to My dear ones I say little; I hang there afresh beside each one through the hours of the heart's agony.

Have you ever thought of the joy that the patient, gentle, loving obedience of My disciples brings to My heart?

# YOU WILL CONQUER

*I Am That I Am: and he said, Thus shalt thou say unto the children of Israel, I Am hath sent me unto you.*

**EXODUS 3:14**

You will conquer. You can never fear changes when I, your Lord, change not. Jesus Christ, the same yesterday, today, and forever. I am beside you. Steadfastness comes to you as you dwell with Me.

Life is a training school. Remember, only the pupil giving great promise of future good work would be so singled out by the Master for strenuous and unwearied discipline, teaching, and training.

# COMPLAIN NOT—LAUGH

*Serve the LORD with gladness. . . . Be thankful unto him, and bless his name.*

## PSALM 100:2, 4

Trust in Me. Do as I say each moment, and all indeed shall be well. Follow My commands: Divine control, unquestioning obedience—these are the only conditions of supply being ample for your own needs and those of others.

Have no fear; go forward. Joy—radiant joy must be yours. Change all disappointment, even if only momentary, into joy. Change each complaint into laughter.

# Too Much Talk

*Study to be quiet.*

1 Thessalonians 4:11

Union with Me is the one great overwhelming necessity. All else follows so naturally, and union with Me may be the result of just consciousness of My presence. Be not too ready to speak to others.

Pray always that the need may be apparent, if you are to do this, and the guidance very plain. My Spirit has been driven out by the words of men.

Discourage too much talk.

Man will see Me in My works done through you.

# I Go Before

*I give unto them eternal life; and they shall never perish.*

### John 10:28

The man who reaches the mountain height by the help of train or car has learned no climber's lesson. But remember this does not mean no guide—this does not mean that My Spirit is not supplying wisdom and strength. How often, when sometimes you little know it, do I go before you to prepare the way, to soften a heart here, to overrule there.

# BLESS YOUR ENEMIES

*But I say unto you, Love your enemies, bless them that curse you,*

*do good to them that hate you, and pray for them*

*which despitefully use you, and persecute you.*

MATTHEW 5:44

Say often, "God bless. . ." of any whom you find in disharmony with you or whom you desire to help. Say it, willing that showers of blessings and joy and success may fall upon them.

Leave to Me the necessary correcting or training; you must only desire joy and blessing for them. At present your prayers are that they should be taught and corrected.

# I Make the Opportunities

*When they deliver you up, take no thought how or what ye shall speak:*
*for it shall be given you in that same hour what ye shall speak.*

### Matthew 10:19

My work in the world has been hindered by work, work, work. Many a tireless, nervous body has driven a spirit. The spirit should be the master always, and just simply and naturally use the body as need should arise. Rest in Me. Do not seek to work for Me. Never make opportunities. Live with Me and for Me. I do the work and I make the opportunities.

# SEEING CHRIST

*Jesus saith unto him, Thomas, because thou hast seen me, thou hast believed:*
*blessed are they that have not seen, and yet have believed.*

## JOHN 20:29

When man sees Me with his human sight, it does not mean of necessity that his spiritual perception is greater. Nay, rather that for that soul I have to span the physical and the spiritual with a spiritual vision clear to human eyes. Remember this to cheer My disciples who have never seen Me and yet have had a clear spiritual consciousness of Me.

# THE ROUNDABOUT WAY

*Rejoice with me; for I have found my sheep which was lost.*

LUKE 15:6

Through briars, through waste places, through glades, up mountain heights, down into valleys, I lead. But ever with the leadership goes the helping hand.

Glorious to follow where your Master goes. But remember that the varied path does not always mean that you need the varied training.

We are seeking lost sheep—we are bringing the kingdom into places where it has not been known before. So realize that you are joining Me on My undying quest—tracking down souls.

# DISHARMONY

*Ask, and it shall be given you; seek, and ye shall find;*

*knock, and it shall be opened unto you.*

### LUKE 11:9

The difficulties of life are caused by disharmony in the individual. There is no discord in My kingdom, only a something unconquered in My disciples. The rule of My kingdom is perfect order, harmony, supply, love, honesty, obedience.

But so often My servants lack power in these and think I fail in My promises because they are not manifested in their lives.

These are but the outward manifestations that result from the obedience, honesty, order, love.

**30**
APRIL

# SPRINGTIME

*Thou hast put gladness in my heart, more than in the time*

*that their corn and their wine increased.*

PSALM 4:7

Rejoice in the springtime of the year. Let there be springtime in your hearts. The full time of fruit is not yet, but there is the promise of the blossom.

Know surely that your life, too, is full of glad promise. Such blessings are to be yours.

All is indeed well. Live in My sunshine and My love.

# Delay Is Not Denial

*As the heavens are higher than the earth, so are my ways higher than your*

*ways, and my thoughts than your thoughts.*

### Isaiah 55:9

Delay is but the all-loving restraint of your Father.

Your life is so linked up with those of others that to let your

desire have instant fulfillment might in many cases cause

another, just as earnest prayer to go unanswered.

Delay is not denial—not even withholding. It is the

opportunity for God to work out your problems and

accomplish your desires in the most wonderful way possible

for you.

# SOULS THAT SMILE

*Be ye kind one to another, tenderhearted, forgiving one another,*

*even as God for Christ's sake hath forgiven you.*

**EPHESIANS 4:32**

The answer to the desire of My disciples to follow Me was "Be ye therefore perfect, even as your Father which is in heaven is perfect."

To accomplish much, be much. In all cases the doing, to be well-doing, must be the mere unconscious expression of the being.

Let the day be full of little prayers to Me, little turnings toward Me. The smiles of the soul at One it loves.

# Kill Self Now

*Knowing this, that our old man is crucified with him, that the body of*

*sin might be destroyed, that henceforth we should not serve sin.*

Romans 6:6

Self dethroned—that is the lesson, but in its place put love for Me, knowledge of Me.

Cease trying to forgive those who fretted or wronged you. It is a mistake to think about it. Aim at killing the self now, in your daily life, and then you will find there is nothing that even remembers injury, because the only one injured, the self, is dead.

# SHARE WITH ME

*Be careful for nothing; but in every thing by prayer and supplication*
*with thanksgiving let your requests be made known unto God.*

## PHILIPPIANS 4:6

I am your Lord, your Creator. I am the same yesterday, today, and forever.

Joy in Me, trust in Me, share all life with Me, see Me in everything, rejoice in Me. Share all with Me as a child shares his pains and cuts and griefs and newfound treasures and joys and little work with his mother.

And give Me the joy of sharing all with you.

# Let Me Choose

*Behold, as the eyes of servants look unto the hand of their masters,*

*and as the eyes of a maiden unto the hand of her mistress;*

*so our eyes wait upon the LORD our God.*

**PSALM 123:2**

Breathe in My very Spirit in fervent desire.

Keep the eye of your spirit ever upon Me, the window of your soul open toward Me. You have ever to know that all things are yours—that what is lovely I delight to give you. Leave more and more the choice to Me. You will have no regrets.

# SUBLIME AUDACITY

*Whosoever shall give to drink unto one of these little ones a cup of cold*

*water. . .verily I say unto you, he shall in no wise lose his reward.*

MATTHEW 10:42

Whatever the world is feeling, I must feel. You are My followers—so the weariness of man today must be shared by you. The weary and heavy-laden must come to you and find that rest that you found in Me.

Poor world—teach it that there is only one cure for all its ills—union with Me. Be filled with My sublime audacity.

# AGAINST THE TIDE

*For it is God which worketh in you both to will*
*and to do of his good pleasure.*

## PHILIPPIANS 2:13

The oarsman, trusting in Me, does not lean on his oars and drift with the tide, trusting the current.

Nay, more often—once I have shown the way—it is against the tide you must direct all your effort. And even when difficulties come, it is by your effort that they will be surmounted. But always strength and the joy in the doing you can have through Me.

# THE REST OF GOD

*In that day there shall be a root of Jesse. . .and his rest shall be glorious.*

### ISAIAH 11:10

I can work through you better when you are at rest. Go very slowly, very quietly, from one duty to the next—taking time to rest and pray between.

Do not be too busy.

Know that you can do all things through Christ who strengthens you. Nay, more, know that you can do all things through Christ who rests you.

# HARMONY WITHIN

*Humble yourselves therefore under the mighty hand of God,*

*that he may exalt you in due time.*

### 1 PETER 5:6

You must not expect to live in a world where all is harmony, where others are in unbroken accord with you. It is your task to maintain your own heart-peace in adverse circumstances. Harmony is always yours when you strain your ear to catch heaven's music.

Doubt always your power or wisdom to put things right; ask Me to right all as you leave it to Me. Only My wisdom can rightly settle any problem.

# CALM—NOT SPEED

*Stand ye in the ways, and see, and ask for the old paths, where is the good way, and walk therein, and ye shall find rest for your souls.*

### JEREMIAH 6:16

All agitation is destructive of good. All calm is constructive of good, and at the same time destructive of evil.

When man wants evil destroyed, so often he rushes to action. It is wrong. First be still and know that I am God. Then act only as I tell you.

Never be afraid of any circumstances or difficulties that help you to cultivate this calm.

# THE DIVINE THIRD

*If two of you shall agree on earth as touching any thing that they shall ask,*

*it shall be done for them of my Father which is in heaven.*

MATTHEW 18:19

When I have led you through these storms, there will be
other words for you, other messages—other guidance.

So great is your desire to love and follow and serve Me that
soon, when this time of difficulty is over, to be alone will
always mean to be shut in with Me.

# THRILL OF PROTECTION

*O thou of little faith, wherefore didst thou doubt?*

MATTHEW 14:31

Turn out all thoughts of doubt and of trouble. Never tolerate them for one second.

Face each day with love and laughter. Face the storm.

Joy, peace, love, My great gifts. Follow Me to find all three. I want you to feel the thrill of protection and safety now. Any soul can feel this in a harbor, but real joy and victory come to those alone who sense these when they ride a storm.

# Never Judge

*Judge not, that ye be not judged.*

## Matthew 7:1

Never judge. The heart of man is so delicate, so complex, only its Maker can know it. Each heart is so different, actuated by different motives, controlled by different circumstances, influenced by different sufferings.

How can one judge of another? Leave to Me the unraveling of the puzzles of life. Leave to Me the teaching of understanding. Bring each heart to Me, its Maker, and leave it with Me, secure in the certainty that all that is wrong I can set right.

# THE LOVE OF A LOVER

*Tell me, O thou whom my soul loveth, where thou feedest,*

*where thou makest thy flock to rest at noon.*

SONG OF SOLOMON 1:7

Yield in all things to My tender insistence, but remember I yield, too, to yours. Ask not only the big things I have told you, but ask the little tender signs of love. Never think of My love as only a tender compassion and forgiveness. It is that, but it is also the love of a lover, who shows His love by countless words and actions and by tender thought.

# FIRST THE SPIRITUAL

*The Spirit of the Lord is upon me, because. . .he hath sent me to heal the*

*brokenhearted, to preach deliverance to the captives. . .*

*to set at liberty them that are bruised.*

LUKE 4:18

"Seek ye first the kingdom of God, and his righteousness; and all these things shall be added unto you."

You would think the material things first and then grow into the knowledge of spiritual things. Not so in My kingdom. It is spiritual things first and then material. So to attain the material, redouble your efforts to acquire the spiritual.

# Pray and Praise

*Men ought always to pray, and not to faint.*

## Luke 18:1

Never weary in prayer. When one day man sees how marvelously his prayer has been answered, then he will deeply regret that he prayed so little.

Pray until you almost cease to pray, because trust has become so rocklike, and then pray on because it has become so much a habit that you cannot resist it.

And always pray until prayer merges into praise. That is the only note on which true prayer should end.

# SORROW TO JOY

*I would not have you to be ignorant, brethren, concerning them which are asleep, that ye sorrow not, even as others which have no hope.*

**1 THESSALONIANS 4:13**

"Weeping may endure for a night, but joy cometh in the morning."

My bravest are those who can anticipate the morning and feel in the night of sorrow that underlying joy that tells of confident expectations of the morning.

# New and Vital Power

*Every one. . .when he looketh upon it, shall live.*

## Numbers 21:8

"Look unto me, and be ye saved, all the ends of the earth." To look is surely within the power of everyone. One look suffices. Salvation follows.

Look and you are saved from despair. Look and you are saved from care. Look and you are saved from worry. Look, and into you there flows a peace beyond all understanding, a power new and vital, a joy wonderful indeed.

# RESCUED AND GUIDED

*He brought me up also out of an horrible pit, out of the miry clay,*

*and set my feet upon a rock.*

### PSALM 40:2

Rest knowing all is safe in My Hands. Rest is trust. Without the knowledge that I am working for you, you do not rest. Lay hold of the truth, pray it, affirm it, hold on to the rope. How foolish are your attempts to save yourself, one hand on the rope, and one making efforts to swim ashore! You may relinquish your hold of the rope and hinder the rescuer.

# WIN ME—WIN ALL

*Only be thou strong and very courageous.*

## JOSHUA 1:7

You will conquer. The conquering spirit is never crushed. Keep a brave and trusting heart. Face all your difficulties in the spirit of conquest.

Rise to greater heights than you have known before. Remember where I am is victory. Forces of evil, within and without you, flee at My presence.

Win Me and all is won. All.

# Fling It at My Feet

*The cares of this world, and the deceitfulness of riches, and the lusts of other things entering in, choke the word, and it becometh unfruitful.*

## Mark 4:19

To see Me you must bring Me your cares and show Me your heart of trust. Then, as you leave your cares, you become conscious of My presence.

This consciousness persisted in brings its reward of Me. Through a mist of care, no man may see My face. Only when the burden is flung at My feet do you pass on to spiritual sight.

# COMMAND YOUR LORD

*Therefore I say unto you, What things soever ye desire, when ye pray,*

*believe that ye receive them, and ye shall have them.*

### MARK 11:24

You are no longer servants but friends. A friend can command his friend—can know that all the true friend has is his by right.

True friendship implies the right to appropriate. You are joint heirs with Me in the inheritance. We share the Father's property. You have the same right to use and claim as I have. Use your right. A beggar supplicates. A son, a daughter, appropriates.

# LITTLE FRETS

*Take us the foxes, the little foxes, that spoil the vines:*

*for our vines have tender grapes.*

**SONG OF SOLOMON 2:15**

Your lack of control is due not to the big burdens, but to your permitting the little frets and cares and burdens to accumulate.

If anything vexes you, deal with that and get that righted with Me before you allow yourself to speak to or meet anybody, or to undertake any new duty.

Look upon yourself more as performing My errands and coming back quickly to tell Me that message is delivered, that task done.

# ABUNDANCE

*Not that we are sufficient of ourselves to think any thing as of ourselves;*

*but our sufficiency is of God.*

2 CORINTHIANS 3:5

Get a feeling of bounteous giving into your being.

I give with a large hand and heart. Note the draught of fishes. The net broke; the boat began to sink with the lavishness of My gift. Lose sight of all limitations.

Abundance is God's supply. Turn out all limited thoughts. Receive showers and in your turn—shower.

# ACCOMPLISH ANYTHING

*Jesus said unto them. . . If ye have faith as a grain of mustard seed. . .*

*nothing shall be impossible unto you.*

**MATTHEW 17:20**

There will be no limit to what you can accomplish.

Think of the tiny snowdrop-shoot in the hard ground. No certainty even that when it has forced its weary way up, sunlight and warmth will greet it.

What a task beyond its power that must seem. But the inner urge of life within the seed compelling it, it carries out that task. The kingdom of heaven is like unto this.

# Claim More

*Hitherto have ye asked nothing in my name: ask, and ye shall receive,*
*that your joy may be full.*

John 16:24

You are doing your claiming as I have said, and soon you will see the result. You cannot do this long without it being seen in the material.

You see others manifesting so easily, so readily demonstrating My power. But you have not seen the discipline that went before. Discipline is absolutely necessary before this power is given to My disciples. It is a further initiation.

# ROOTS AND FRUITS

*As ye have therefore received Christ Jesus the Lord, so walk ye in him:*

*rooted and built up in him.*

### COLOSSIANS 2:6–7

Remember the lesson of the seed in its sending a shoot down so that it may be rooted and grounded, while at the same time it sends a shoot up to be the plant that gladdens the world.

The two growths are necessary. Without the strong root it would soon wither, as much activity fails for lack of growth in Me. The higher the growth up, the deeper must be the enrooting.

# TEST YOUR LOVE

*Godliness with contentment is great gain.*

1 TIMOTHY 6:6

A great love knows that in every difficulty, every trial, every failure, the presence of the loved one suffices. Test your love for Me by this.

Just to be with Me, just to know I am beside you—does that bring you joy and peace? If not, then your love for Me, and your realization of My love, are at fault.

Then, if this be so, pray for more love.

# FORGET

*This one thing I do, forgetting those things which are behind. . .I press*
*toward the mark for the prize of the high calling of God in Christ Jesus.*

### PHILIPPIANS 3:13–14

Regret nothing. Not even the sins and failures. When a man
views earth's wonders from some mountain height he does
not spend his time dwelling on the stones and stumbles, the
faints and failures, that marked his upward path.

So with you. Breathe in the rich blessings of each new
day—forget all that lies behind you.

# The Devil's Death Knell

*Whoso offereth praise glorifieth me.*

### Psalm 50:23

Praise is the devil's death knell. Resignation, acceptance of My will, obedience to it, have not the power to vanquish evil that praise has.

The joyful heart is My best weapon against all evil. Oh! Pray and praise.

Go with songs of rejoicing. Rejoice.

Talk to Me more during the day. Look up into My face— a look of love, a feeling of security, a thrill of joy at the sense of the nearness of My presence—these are your best prayers.

# Prayer without Words

*Pray without ceasing.*

1 Thessalonians 5:17

Spend much time in prayer. Prayer is the linking up of the soul and mind and heart to God.

So that if it is only a glance of faith, a look or word of love, or confidence, and no supplication is expressed, it yet follows that supply and all necessary are secured.

Because the soul, being linked to God, united to Him, receives in and through Him all things. And the soul, when in human form, needs, too, the things belonging to its habitation.

# COMPANIONSHIP

*I am my beloved's, and my beloved is mine.*

## SONG OF SOLOMON 6:3

The way of the soul's transformation is the way of divine companionship.

Not so much the asking Me to make you this or that but the living with Me, thinking of Me, talking to Me—thus you grow like Me.

Love Me. Rest in Me. Joy in Me.

# MY IMAGE

*For whom he did foreknow, he also did predestinate
to be conformed to the image of his Son.*

ROMANS 8:29

You are willing to drink of the cup that I drink of—the wine of sorrow and disappointment.

You are Mine and will grow more and more like Me, your Master.

True it is today as it was in the days of Moses that no man can see My face and live.

The self, the original man, shrivels up and dies, and upon the soul becomes stamped My image.

# Eject Sin with Love

*Owe no man any thing, but to love one another:*
*for he that loveth another hath fulfilled the law.*

Romans 13:8

Love is the power that transforms the world. Love not only of Me, love not only of the few dear to you, but love of all—of the publicans, the sinners, the harlots.

It is the only weapon with which sin can be driven out. Drive sin out with love.

Drive fear and depression and despair and a sense of failure out with praise.

# DIVINE PATIENCE

*The vessel that he made of clay was marred in the hand of the potter: so he made it again another vessel, as seemed good to the potter to make it.*

## JEREMIAH 18:4

Shortcomings you had hardly recognized or at least for which you had had no sense of sorrow now cause you trouble and dismay.

That is in itself a sign of progress.

As you see your slow progress upward, in spite of your longing and struggle, you will gain a divine patience with others whose imperfections trouble you.

# THAT TENDER VOICE

*And after the wind an earthquake; but the Lord was not in the earthquake:*

*and after the earthquake a fire; but the Lord was not in the fire:*

*and after the fire a still small voice.*

### 1 KINGS 19:11–12

Listen to My voice. Never heed the voices of the world—only the tender divine voice.

Listen, and anxious thoughts and tired nerves will become rested.

The tenderness and the restfulness will heal your scars and make you strong, and then it must be your task to let all your power be My power.

# HOW MEN SEE ME

*My God shall supply all your need according to his riches*

*in glory by Christ Jesus.*

PHILIPPIANS 4:19

I came to help a world. And according to the varying needs of each, so does each man see Me.

The weak need My strength. The strong need My tenderness. The tempted and fallen need My salvation. The righteous need My pity for sinners. The lonely need a friend. The fighters need a leader.

No man could be all these to men—only a God could be.

# TRUE BEAUTY

*Let the beauty of the LORD our God be upon us:*

*and establish thou the work of our hands upon us.*

PSALM 90:17

Not only live, but grow in grace and power and the beauty of holiness.

Reach ever forward after the things of My kingdom.

In the animal world the very form of an animal alters to enable it to reach that upon which it delights to feed.

So reaching after the treasures of My kingdom your whole nature becomes changed, so that you can best enjoy and receive the wonders of that kingdom.

# THE ONLY WAY

*The very God of peace sanctify you wholly; and I pray God your whole*

*spirit and soul and body be preserved blameless unto the coming*

*of our Lord Jesus Christ.*

1 THESSALONIANS 5:23

Down through the ages My power alone has kept millions of souls brave and true and strong who else would have fallen by the way.

This life is not for the body; it is for the soul, and man too often chooses the way of life that best suits the body, not the soul. I permit only what best suits the soul.

# An Obstacle Race

*I keep under my body, and bring it into subjection: lest that by any means, when I have preached to others, I myself should be a castaway.*

1 Corinthians 9:27

Your discipleship is an obstacle race. "So run that ye may obtain." Obtain not only your heart's desires, but obtain Me—your soul's joy and haven.

What would you think of the runner who threw himself on the ground in despondency at his first hurdle?

Over and on and up. I am your leader and your goal.

# The Day of Trouble

*By him therefore let us offer the sacrifice of praise to God continually, that is, the fruit of our lips giving thanks to his name.*

### Hebrews 13:15

The world wonders when it sees the man who can so unexpectedly draw large sums from his bank.

But what the world has not seen are the countless small sums paid into that bank, earned by faithful work in many ways.

So in My kingdom. The world sees the man of faith make a sudden demand upon Me, upon My stores, and lo! that demand is met.

# MY MARK!

*The fruit of the Spirit is love, joy, peace. . . .*

GALATIANS 5:22

That is the peace that only I can give in the midst of a restless world. To know that peace is to have received the stamp of the kingdom—the mark of the Lord Jesus Christ. When you have learned that peace, you are fit to judge of the values of the kingdom, and the values of all the world has to offer.

# HOUSE ON A ROCK

*Therefore now amend your ways and your doings,*

*and obey the voice of the LORD your God.*

### JEREMIAH 26:13

I likened the man who obeyed Me implicitly to the man who built his house upon a rock. In times of storm he is steadfast, immovable.

The secure, steadfast, immovable life of My disciples is not built at a wish, in a moment, but is laid, stone by stone, foundations, walls, roof, by the acts of obedience, the daily following out of My wishes, the loving doing of My will.

# GOD-INSPIRED

*Look not every man on his own things,*

*but every man also on the things of others.*

## PHILIPPIANS 2:4

You have entered now upon a mountain climb. Steep steps lead upward, but your power to help others will be truly marvelous.

Not alone will you arise. All toward whom you now send loving, pitying thoughts will be helped upward by you.

When you look to Me, all your thoughts are God-inspired. Act on them and you will be led on. They are not your own impulses but the movement of My Spirit and, obeyed, will bring the answer to your prayers.

# FACE TODAY WITH ME

*Lead me in thy truth, and teach me: for thou art the God of my salvation;*

*on thee do I wait all the day.*

**PSALM 25:5**

It is not circumstances that need altering first, but yourselves, and then the conditions will naturally alter. Spare no effort to become all I would have you.

Endeavor to put from you every thought of trouble. Take each day, and with no backward look, face the day's problem with Me, and seek My help and guidance as to what you can do.

# "Glory, Glory Dawneth"

*When he, the Spirit of truth, is come, he will guide you into all truth. . .*

*he will shew you things to come.*

### John 16:13

I am planning for you. Wonderful are My ways beyond your knowledge.

Realize My bounty and My goodness more and more. The wonder of being led by Me! The beauty of a guided life!

You are overcoming. You are counting all things but loss if you can win Me. And the promises to him who overcomes are truly wonderful and will always be fulfilled.

# Seek Me Early

*Whoso hearkeneth unto me shall dwell safely,*

*and shall be quiet from fear of evil.*

### Proverbs 1:33

The world flies to Me when its difficulties are too great to be surmounted any other way, forgetting, or never realizing, that if those hearts sought Me, many of the difficulties would not arise.

The circumstances, the life, the character would be so altered that those same difficulties would not exist.

Seek Me early; that is the way to find Me. Early, before I get crowded out by life's troubles and difficulties and pleasures.

# DEAR NAME

*She shall bring forth a son, and thou shalt call his name JESUS:*

*for he shall save his people from their sins.*

### MATTHEW 1:21

Say My name often.

"Jesus." The very sounding of My name drives away all evil.

"Jesus." My name is the call for a lifeline to rescue you from temptation.

"Jesus." The name banishes loneliness—dispels gloom.

"Jesus." Summons help to conquer your faults.

I will set you on high because you have known My name.

Yes! My name—"Jesus." Use it more. Use it tenderly. Use it prayerfully. Use it powerfully.

# WAIT

*It came to pass, that, as he was praying in a certain place. . .*

*one of his disciples said unto him, Lord, teach us to pray.*

**LUKE 11:1**

The world has always seen service for Me to be activity. Only those near to Me have seen that a life of prayer may, and does so often, accomplish more than all the service man can offer Me.

If man lived apart with Me and only went out to serve at My direct command, My Spirit could operate more and accomplish truly mighty things.

# THE SUCCESS YOU COVET

*For your obedience is come abroad unto all men.*

## ROMANS 16:19

Follow the path of obedience. It leads to the throne of God. Your treasure—be it success necessary on the material plane, which will further the work of My kingdom, or the hidden spiritual wonders revealed by Me to those only who diligently seek—this treasure lies at the end of the track. From one point (a promise of Mine or a command) to the next, you have to follow, till finally you reach the success you covet.

# MIRACLES AGAIN

*There shall no evil befall thee, neither shall any plague*

*come nigh thy dwelling.*

## PSALM 91:10

Wait to hear My will and then obey. At all costs obey.

Do not fear. I am a wall of protection around you. To see this

with the eyes of faith is to cause it to manifest in the material.

Remember I long to work miracles, as when on earth I

wrought them, but the same condition holds good. I cannot

do many mighty works because of unbelief.

So only in response to your belief can I do miracle-

works now.

# SEE AS I SEE

*Take my yoke upon you, and learn of me; for I am meek and lowly in heart:*
*and ye shall find rest unto your souls. For my yoke is easy,*
*and my burden is light.*

## MATTHEW 11:29–30

Learn of Me. The only way for so many in My poor world to keep sane is to have the mind that is in Jesus Christ.

That mind you can never obtain by reasoning, or by reading, but only by living with Me and sharing My life.

Think much of Me. See others as I see them.

# Your Red Sea

*The wicked flee when no man pursueth: but the righteous are bold as a lion.*

## Proverbs 28:1

Go forward fearlessly.

Do not think about the Red Sea that lies ahead.

Be very sure that when you come to it the waters will part and you will pass over to your promised land of freedom.

# CLING TO ME

*He said unto them, Come ye yourselves apart into a desert place,*
*and rest a while.*

**MARK 6:31**

Cling to Me until the life from Me, the divine life, by that very contact, flows into your being and revives your fainting spirit.

Become recharged. When weary, do as I did on earth—sit by the well. Rest.

Rest and gain power and strength, and the work, too, will come to you as it came to Me.

Rest till every care-thought has gone, and then let the tide of love and joy flow in.

# WHEN GUIDANCE TARRIES

*Thou shalt guide me with thy counsel, and afterward receive me to glory.*

**PSALM 73:24**

As I prompt you—act. When you have no clear guidance, then go forward quietly along the path of duty I have set before you.

No fear, no panic, quietly doing your daily duty.

This attitude of faith will receive its reward, as surely as the acting upon My direct guidance.

Rejoice in the sense of security that is yours.

# God's Friendship

*Who hath despised the day of small things?*

### Zechariah 4:10

I am your friend. The companion of the dreary ways of life. I rob those ways of their grayness and horror. I transform them.

Have you ever realized the wonder of the friendship you can have with Me? Have you ever thought what it means to be able to summon at will the God of the world?

To My subjects I have given the right to enter My presence when they will; nay, more, they can summon Me— and I am there.

# DO NOT RUSH

*They soon forgat his works; they waited not for his counsel.*

**PSALM 106:13**

Learn in the little daily things of life to delay action until you get My guidance.

So many lives lack poise. For in the momentous decisions and the big things of life, they ask My help, but into the small things they rush alone.

By what you do in the small things, those around you are most often antagonized or attracted.

# NO SELF-REPROACH

*There is therefore now no condemnation to them which are in Christ Jesus,*
*who walk not after the flesh, but after the Spirit.*

## ROMANS 8:1

I had no words of reproach for any I healed. The man was
whole and free who had wrecked his physical being by sin.
The woman taken in adultery was told, "Neither do I
condemn thee: go, and sin no more." She was not told to bear
the burden of the consciousness of her sin.

Faith is your attitude toward Me. Charity your attitude
toward your fellow man, but as necessary is hope.

# TABLE OF DELIGHTS

*All the days of the afflicted are evil: but he that is of*

*a merry heart hath a continual feast.*

## PROVERBS 15:15

Life is flooded through and through with joy and gladness.
Indeed, I have prepared a table of delights, a feast of all good
things for you.

Indeed, your cup runs over and you can feel from the
very depth of your heart: "Surely goodness and mercy shall
follow me all the days of my life: and I will dwell in the house
of the LORD for ever."

# My Will—Your Joy

*The Lord is thy keeper: the Lord is thy shade upon thy right hand.*

## Psalm 121:5

You can never go beyond My love and care. Circumstances I bless and use must be the right ones for you.

But the first step is to lay your will before Me as an offering, sure that if you trust Me, what I do for you will be best.

Your second step is to be sure that I am powerful enough to do everything, that no miracle is impossible with Me.

Then leave all with Me.

# UNDERSTAND THEM

*The kingdom of heaven is like unto treasure. . .which when a man hath*
*found, he hideth, and for joy thereof goeth and selleth all that he hath,*
*and buyeth that field.*

### MATTHEW 13:44

Always seek to understand others and you cannot fail to love
them.

See Me in the dull, the uninteresting, the sinful, the
critical, the miserable.

See Me in the laughter of children and the sweetness of
old age, in the courage of youth and the patience of man- and
womanhood.

# ATTACK FEAR

*Moses said. . .Fear ye not, stand still, and see the salvation of the L*ORD*,*

*which he will shew to you to day.*

EXODUS 14:13

Do not fear. Remember how I faced the devil in the wilderness and how I conquered with "the sword of the Spirit, which is the word of God." You, too, have your quick answer for every fear that evil may present—an answer of faith and confidence in Me. Where possible say it aloud. Look on every fear as a very real temptation to be attacked and overthrown.

# THE CHILD-SPIRIT

*Jesus called a little child unto him. . .and said. . .Except ye be converted, and*
*become as little children, ye shall not enter into the kingdom of heaven.*

MATTHEW 18:2–3

Seek in every way to become childlike. Not only for its simple
trust must you copy the child-spirit, but for its joy in life, its
ready laughter, its lack of criticism, its desire to share all with
all men. Ask much that you may become as little children,
friendly and loving towards all—not critical, not fearful.

# SPIRITUAL FULLNESS

*As the hart panteth after the water brooks,*

*so panteth my soul after thee, O God.*

**PSALM 42:1**

"Blessed are they which do hunger and thirst after

righteousness: for they shall be filled." That is satisfaction.

Only in that fullness of spiritual things can the heartsick and

faint and weary be satisfied, healed, and rested.

How few realize that the feeding of the four thousand

and the five thousand was in each case but an illustration of

the way in which I should one day be the food of My people.

# Friend of Mine

*A man that hath friends must shew himself friendly: and there is a friend that sticketh closer than a brother.*

## Proverbs 18:24

What man calls conversion is often only the discovery of the great Friend. What man calls religion is the knowledge of the great Friend.

I am your friend. Think of all that means. A friend is ready to help, anticipating every want, hand outstretched to help and encourage or to ward off danger, voice of tenderness to soothe tired nerves and speak peace to restlessness and fear.

# YOU ARE INVINCIBLE

*He shall deliver their kings into thine hand, and thou shalt destroy their name from under heaven: there shall no man be able to stand before thee.*

## DEUTERONOMY 7:24

To the passenger it may seem as if each wave would overwhelm the ship or turn it aside from its course. The captain knows by experience that in spite of wind and wave, he steers a straight course to the haven where he would be. So trust Me, the captain of your salvation.

# Riches

*Wealth and riches shall be in his house:*

*and his righteousness endureth for ever.*

Never let yourself think, "We cannot afford this," or "We shall never be able to do that." Say, "The supply for it is not here yet, but it will come if we should have it. It will surely come."

Persevere in saying that and gradually a feeling of being plentifully supplied and of being surrounded by riches will possess you. That feeling is your faith claiming My supply, and according to your faith it shall be unto you.

# PAINFUL PREPARATION

*Beloved, think it not strange concerning the fiery trial which is to try you. . .but rejoice, inasmuch as ye are partakers of Christ's sufferings.*

1 PETER 4:12–13

Painful as this time is, you will one day see the reason of it, and see, too, that it was not cruel testing, but tender preparation for the wonderful lifework you are to do.

Try to realize that your own prayers are being most wonderfully answered. Answered in a way that seems painful to you but that just now is the only way.

*God Calling*

8

JULY

# My Secret

*Jesus saith unto them, My meat is to do the will of him that sent me,*
*and to finish his work.*

John 4:34

You are being guided, but remember that I said, "I will guide thee with Mine eye."

And My eye is My set purpose—My will.

To guide with My will is to bring all your desires into oneness with My will, My desires.

To make My will your only will. Then My will may guide you.

# WHY DOUBT?

*Let all those that put their trust in thee rejoice: let them ever shout for*

*joy, because thou defendest them: let them also that love thy name*

*be joyful in thee.*

PSALM 5:11

Trust and pray. It is not sin for one who knows Me only as God to doubt Me, to question My love and purposes.

But for one who knows Me as you do, as friend and Savior, and who knows the world's God as Father—for that one to doubt My purpose and saving power and tender love is wrong indeed.

# EXPECT MANY MIRACLES

*This beginning of miracles did Jesus in Cana of Galilee, and manifested forth his glory; and his disciples believed on him.*

## JOHN 2:11

My guardianship is so wonderful.

Expect not one miracle but many.

Each day's happenings, if of My working and under My control, are miracle-works.

# Guardian Angels

*I will praise thee; for I am fearfully and wonderfully made.*

## Psalm 139:14

You are Mine. Once I have set on you My stamp and seal of ownership, all My hosts throng to serve and protect you.

Try to picture a bodyguard of My servitors in the unseen waiting, longing, efficient to do all that is necessary for your well-being.

Feel this as you go through the day. Feel this and all is well.

# Savior and Savior

*Being confident of this very thing, that he which hath begun a good work in you will perform it until the day of Jesus Christ.*

## Philippians 1:6

Even a human rescuer does not save a man from drowning only to place him in other deep and dangerous waters. But rather to place him on dry land and there to restore him to animation and health and to see him to his home.

From this parable learn what I your rescuer would do, and even more. Is the Lord's hand shortened that it cannot save?

# EXPECT THE GOOD

*So then faith cometh by hearing, and hearing by the word of God.*

## ROMANS 10:17

Can you get the expectant attitude of faith? Not waiting for the next evil to befall you but awaiting with a child's joyful trust the next good in store?

# True Success

*Every place that the sole of your foot shall tread upon,*

*that have I given unto you, as I said unto Moses.*

### Joshua 1:3

Rejoice indeed that you see My hand in all the happenings
and the keepings of the day. Protected, the Israelites crossed
the Red Sea; so are you protected in all things.

Rely on this and go forward. You have now entered
upon the stage of success. You must not doubt this. It is true.
It is sure.

# SONGS ON THE WAY

*Thou art my hiding place; thou shalt preserve me from trouble; thou shalt compass me about with songs of deliverance.*

### PSALM 32:7

Many of My disciples have had to stay on in the dark, alone and friendless, singing as they went.

For you, too, there must be songs on the way. Should I plant your feet on an insecure ladder? Its supports may be out of your sight, hidden in the secret place of the Most High, but if I have asked you to step up firmly—then surely have I secured your ladder.

# REFUGE

*In the time of trouble he shall hide me in his pavilion:*

*in the secret of his tabernacle shall he hide me.*

### PSALM 27:5

Know My divine power. Trust in Me. Dwell in My love. Laugh and trust. Laughter is a child's faith in God and good.

Seek safety in My secret place. You cannot be touched or harmed there. That is sure.

Really feel as if you were in a strong tower, strongly guarded, and against which nothing can prevail.

# PEACE, BE STILL

*He saith unto them, Why are ye fearful, O ye of little faith? Then he
arose, and rebuked the winds and the sea; and there was a great calm.*

MATTHEW 8:26

You are passing through a storm. Enough that I am with you
to say, "Peace, be still," to quiet both winds and waves.

It was on the quiet mountain slopes that I taught My
disciples the truths of My kingdom, not during the storm.
So with you, the time of the mountain slopes will come, and
you shall rest with Me and learn.

# WALK HUMBLY

*Let nothing be done through strife or vainglory; but in lowliness of mind let each esteem other better than themselves.*

## PHILIPPIANS 2:3

Fear of what others will say is want of trust in Me. This must not be. Convert all these difficulties into the purification of your character.

See yourselves as those around you see you, not as you wish to be, and walk very humbly with your God.

I will set you on high because you have known My name, but it must be a purified you to be so exalted.

# Marvelous Happenings

*The LORD is my shepherd; I shall not want.*

### PSALM 23:1

You see a marvelous happening, happening so easily, so simply, so free from all other agency, and you wonder.

This has not happened easily and simply. It has been achieved by hours, days, months of weariness and heartache battled against and overcome, by a steadfast, unflinching desire to conquer self and to do My will and live My teachings.

The frets and the worries and the scorn patiently borne mean spiritual power acquired, operating marvelously.

# My Standard

*I fear, lest by any means, as the serpent beguiled Eve through his subtilty, so your minds should be corrupted from the simplicity that is in Christ.*

2 Corinthians 11:3

Carry out My commands and leave the result to Me. Remember that the commands I have given you have been already worked out by Me in the spirit-world to produce in your case and circumstances the required result. So follow My rules faithfully.

Each individual was meant to walk with Me in this way, to act under divine control, strengthened by divine power.

# THE WAY OF PRAISE

*I will praise thee with my whole heart: before the gods will*

*I sing praise unto thee.*

**PSALM 138:1**

I am teaching you My way of removing mountains. The way to remove mountains is the way of praise. When a trouble comes, think of all you have to be thankful for.

Say "thank You" all the time. This is the remover of mountains, your thankful heart of praise.

# MIRACLE OF THE AGES

*Abide in me, and I in you. As the branch cannot bear fruit of itself, except it abide in the vine; no more can ye, except ye abide in me.*

## JOHN 15:4

"The works that I do shall ye do also; and greater works than these shall ye do; because I go unto My Father."

Greater works! Wonder of the world! God's power manifest in believing man! God's power going out to bless, through the agency of the man actuated by the Holy Spirit.

# STOP ALL WORK UNTIL—

*Great peace have they which love thy law: and nothing shall offend them.*

**PSALM 119:165**

That peace does truly pass all understanding. No man has the power to disturb that peace, but you can let the world and its worries and distractions in.

You can give entrance to fears and despondency.

Allow nothing to disturb your peace with Me. Do not let those about you spoil your peace of heart and mind. Do not let anyone without, any trouble, any irritation, any adversity, disturb it for one moment.

# KEEP CLOSE

*He said, My presence shall go with thee, and I will give thee rest.*

## EXODUS 33:14

Keep close to Me and you shall know the way, because, as I said to My disciples, I am the Way. That is the solution to all earth's problems.

Keep close, very close to Me. Think, act, and live in My presence.

How dare any foe touch you, protected by Me! That is the secret of all power, all peace, all purity, all influence, the keeping very near to Me.

Abide in Me. Rejoice in My love.

# WONDERFUL LIFE

*A man's heart deviseth his way: but the L*ORD* directeth his steps.*

## PROVERBS 16:9

I am your Lord, controller of your days, your present and your future. Leave all plans to Me. Only act as I bid you. You have entered now upon the God-guided life. Think what that means. God-taught, God-guided.

Is anything too wonderful for such a life? Do you begin to see how wonderful life with Me can be?

Do you see that no evil can befall you?

# FORGET—FORGIVE

*Forbearing one another, and forgiving one another, if any man have a quarrel against any: even as Christ forgave you, so also do ye.*

## COLOSSIANS 3:13

Our Lord, we thank Thee for so much.

We bless Thee and praise Thy glorious name.

Fill your world with love and laughter. Never mind what anguish lies behind you.

Forget, forgive, love, and laugh.

Treat all as you would treat Me, with love and consideration.

Let nothing that others do to you alter your treatment of them.

# My Consolation

*I will walk among you, and will be your God, and ye shall be my people.*

## Leviticus 26:12

I walk with you, not only to guide and comfort you, but for solace and comfort for Myself.

When a loving child is by you, is the nearness only that you may provide protection and help for that little one?

Rather, too, that in that little child you may find joy and cheer and comfort in his simplicity, his love, his trust.

So, too, is it in your power to comfort and bring joy to My heart.

# MISTAKES

*After these things the word of the LORD came unto Abram in a vision,*

*saying, Fear not, Abram: I am thy shield, and thy exceeding great reward.*

**GENESIS 15:1**

You wonder sometimes why you are permitted to make mistakes when you sought so truly to do My will in the matter.

To that I say it was no mistake. All your lessons cannot be learned without difficulty, and this was needed to teach you a lesson. Not to him who walks on, with no obstacles in his way, but to him that overcometh is the promise given.

# SUNLIT GLADES

*Jesus saith unto him, If I will that he tarry till I come,*
*what is that to thee? follow thou me.*

JOHN 21:22

Do not think that suffering is the only path into My kingdom. There are sunlit glades and ways amid the loveliest flowers, along which the steps and hearts of men are drawn to Me.

Bleak, cold, and desolate are not all the ways. Leave all to Me. The choice of ways, the guidance in the way. But when the sunlight calls, accept it gladly.

**30**
JULY

# FAITH REWARDED

*For what saith the scripture? Abraham believed God,*
*and it was counted unto him for righteousness.*

**ROMANS 4:3**

Think much of My servants of old. How Abraham believed the promise (when as yet he had no child) that in his seed all the nations of the earth should be blessed.

How Moses led the children of Israel through the desert, sure that at last they would gain the Promised Land.

Down through the ages there have always been those who obeyed, not seeing but believing, and their faith was rewarded. So shall it be with you.

# GRATITUDE

*The trumpeters and singers were as one, to make one sound to be heard in praising and thanking the LORD.*

2 CHRONICLES 5:13

Give Me the gift of a brave and thankful heart.

When life seems hard and troubles crowd, then very definitely look for causes for thankfulness.

The sacrifice, the offering of thanksgiving, is indeed a sweet incense going up to Me through the busy day.

Seek diligently for something to be glad and thankful about in every happening, and soon no search will be required.

# Blessed Bond

*He is our peace, who hath made both one, and hath broken down the*

*middle wall of partition between us.*

**Ephesians 2:14**

"I will never leave thee, nor forsake thee."

There is no bond of union on earth to compare with the union between Me and a soul who loves Me. Priceless beyond all earth's imaginings is that friendship.

In the merging of heart and mind and will, a oneness results that only those who experience it can even dimly realize.

# HARVEST

*So the LORD blessed the latter end of Job more than his beginning.*

JOB 42:12

I love to pour My blessings down in rich measure. But as with the seed-sowing, the ground must be prepared before the seed is dropped in.

Yours to prepare the soil—Mine to drop the seed-blessing into the prepared soil.

Together we share in, and joy in, the harvest.

Spend more time in soil-preparing. Prayer fertilizes soil. There is much to do in preparation.

# GIVE EVERY MOMENT

*Ye shall not go up, nor fight against your brethren the children of Israel:*
*return every man to his house; for this thing is from me.*

1 KINGS 12:24

How dear to my heart is the cry of love that asks for all of
Me. Above all I desire true, warm, childlike love, and then
the gift I prize next is all the moments.

The little things you planned to do, given up gladly at
My suggestion, the little services joyfully rendered. See Me in
all, and then it will be an easy task.

# ETERNAL LIFE

*He that hath the Son hath life; and he that hath*
*not the Son of God hath not life.*

1 JOHN 5:12

Eternal life is the only lasting life, so that all that is done
without being done in the power of My Spirit, My life, is
passing. All done in that Spirit-life is undying.

"I give unto them eternal life; and they shall never
perish, neither shall any man pluck them out of My hand." So
eternal life means security, too, and safety. Dwell increasingly
in the consciousness of that security.

# HOUR OF NEED

*Heal me, O LORD, and I shall be healed; save me,*

*and I shall be saved: for thou art my praise.*

**JEREMIAH 17:14**

I am your healer, your joy, your Lord. You bid Me, your Lord, come. Did you not know that I am here? With noiseless footfall I draw near to you.

Your hour of need is the moment of My coming.

Could you know My love, could you measure My longing to help, you would know that I need no agonized pleading.

Your need is My call.

# DWELL APART

*Be not drunk with wine, wherein is excess; but be filled with the Spirit.*

**EPHESIANS 5:18**

Rest more with Me. If I, the Son of God, needed those times of quiet communion with My Father, alone, away from noise, from activity—then surely you need them, too.

Refilling with the Spirit is a need. That dwelling apart, that shutting yourself away in the very secret place of your being—away alone with Me.

From these times you come forth in power to bless and heal.

# ALL IS WELL

*Oh how great is thy goodness, which thou hast laid up for them that fear*

*thee; which thou hast wrought for them that trust in thee.*

PSALM 31:19

My keeping power is never at fault, but only your realization of it. Not whether I can provide a shelter from the storm, but your failure to be sure of the security of that shelter.

Every fear, every doubt, is a crime against My love.

Oh! Trust. Practice daily, many times a day, saying, "All is well."

Say it until you believe it, know it.

# EMPTY YOURSELF

*I will both lay me down in peace, and sleep: for thou, LORD,*

*only makest me dwell in safety.*

PSALM 4:8

Rely on Me alone. Pay all out in the spirit of trust that more will come to meet your supply.

Empty your vessel quickly to ensure a divine supply.

So much retained by you, so much the less will be gained from Me. It is a law of divine supply.

To hold back, to retain, implies a fear of the future, a want of trust in Me.

Empty your vessel. I will fill it.

# Effort and Rest

*Unto thee, O God, do we give thanks, unto thee do we give thanks:*

*for that thy name is near thy wondrous works declare.*

**Psalm 75:1**

Come to Me, talk to Me, dwell with Me, and then you will know My way is a sure way, My paths are safe paths.

Come very near to Me.

Dig deep down into the soil of the kingdom. Effort and rest—a union of the two.

# STRAY SHEEP

*He. . .fell on his face, and prayed, saying, O my Father, if it be possible,*

*let this cup pass from me: nevertheless not as I will, but as thou wilt.*

### MATTHEW 26:39

For straying there is no cure except to keep so close to Me that nothing can come between us.

Sure of that, you can but stay at My side, knowing that, as I am the very Way itself, nothing can prevent your being in the Way; nothing can cause you to stray.

# YOU ARE MINE

*The righteous is delivered out of trouble, and the wicked cometh in his stead.*

## PROVERBS 11:8

I and My Father are one. So He who made the ordered, beautiful world out of chaos, and set the stars in their courses, and made each plant to know its season, can He not bring out of your little chaos peace and order?

And He and I are one, and you are Mine. Your affairs are Mine. It is My divine task to order My affairs—therefore yours will be ordered by Me.

# RULE THE WORLD

*I thank thee, and praise thee, O thou God of my fathers,*

*who hast given me wisdom and might, and hast made known*

*unto me now what we desired of thee.*

DANIEL 2:23

What is wrong in your country? Think out quietly, and make these matters your prayer matters. You will see lives you never touch altered, laws made at your request, evils banished.

You may never go beyond one room, and yet you may become one of the most powerful forces for good in your country, in the world.

# PERFECTION

*Follow peace with all men, and holiness, without which no man shall see the Lord: looking diligently lest any man fail of the grace of God.*

HEBREWS 12:14–15

Ever your helper through dark to light, through weakness to power, through sin to salvation, through danger to security, through poverty to plenty, through indifference to love, through resentment to perfect forgiveness.

Never be satisfied with a comparison with those around you. Ever let My words ring out. "Be ye therefore perfect, even as your Father which is in heaven is perfect." Stop short at nothing less.

# My Richest Gift

*The water that I shall give him. . .shall be in him a well of water springing up into everlasting life.*

JOHN 4:14

Life—spiritual, mental, physical, abundant, joyous, powerful life. Yes! These I came to give you.

Think you not My heart was sad that so few would accept that gracious gift?

Think! Earth's richest, choicest gift held out—free to all, and no man to care to stretch out a hand to take it.

Is that possible? My gift, that precious gift of abundant life—man turns away from it.

# Not Punishment

*As far as the east is from the west, so far hath he removed*

*our transgressions from us.*

**PSALM 103:12**

I will guide your efforts. You are not being punished for past sins. Take My words, revealed to you each day from the beginning, and do in all things as I say. I have been showing you the way.

I have told you that I am longing to use you.

# NO TIRED WORK

*Jesus went about all Galilee. . .healing all manner of sickness*

*and all manner of disease among the people.*

MATTHEW 4:23

Rest. It is wrong to force work. Rest until eternal life, flowing

through your veins and hearts and minds, bids you bestir

yourselves, and work, glad work, will follow.

Tired work never tells.

Rest. Remember I am your physician, healer of mind

and body.

Look to Me for cure, for rest, for peace.

# NATURE LAUGHS

*Ye shall go out with joy, and be led forth with peace: the mountains and the hills shall break forth before you into singing, and all the trees of the field shall clap their hands.*

ISAIAH 55:12

Sunshine helps to make glad the heart of man. It is the laughter of nature.

Live much outside. My medicines are sun and air, trust and faith. Trust is the spirit sun, your being enwrapped by the divine Spirit.

Faith is the soul's breathing in of the divine Spirit.

Nature is often My nurse for tired souls and weary bodies.

# STONES OF THE WAY

*The law of the Spirit of life in Christ Jesus hath made me*

*free from the law of sin and death.*

ROMANS 8:2

You know the difference between taking a loving child with you when the child accepts naturally each decision as to each turning—and the child who resists and has to be forced.

It is not the way, but the loving rejoicing in the way and the guidance, that matters with My disciples. You are ready for the guidance, but you do not rejoice as you should in the little daily stones of the way.

# A Human Temple

*What? know ye not that your body is the temple of the Holy Ghost which is in you?*

1 Corinthians 6:19

As you kneel in humble adoration, I will tell you that when I took upon Me your humanity, it was with the desire of raising that humanity to My divinity.

Earth gave Me her best—a human temple to enclose My divinity—and I brought to her the possession of divine power, love, strength, to be forever expressed in those of her children who opened their hearts to Me and sought to live My life.

# SHAME AND REMORSE

*They departed. . .rejoicing that they were counted worthy*
*to suffer shame for his name.*

### ACTS 5:41

Peter could never have done My work, but for the tender love with which I enwrapped him. Not from the anger of My Father did I need to protect him. No! But from the hatred of Peter himself.

So to My followers today there come the shame and contempt of themselves.

I lay it on you as a command—no looking back. Remember no more others' sins and failures or your own.

# BROKEN VOICES

*Therefore if any man be in Christ, he is a new creature:*
*old things are passed away; behold, all things are become new.*

2 CORINTHIANS 5:17

Clipped wings can grow again. Broken voices regain a strength and beauty unknown before. Your power to help other lives will soon bring its delight, even when, at first, the help to yourselves may seem too late to bring you joy.

Worn-out and tired as you may seem, and pain-weary, I say unto you, "Behold, I make all things new." That promise shall be fulfilled.

# GLEAMS OF SUNLIGHT

*Rejoice, inasmuch as ye are partakers of Christ's sufferings; that, when his glory shall be revealed, ye may be glad also with exceeding joy.*

1 PETER 4:13

Take your pains and sufferings, difficulties and hardships, each day and offer them up for one troubled soul or for some prayer specially needing to be answered.

Learn from My life of the suffering that saves others. So you will sing in your pain. Across the grayest days there are the gleams of sunlight.

# The Summit

*The Lord God is my strength, and he will make my feet like hinds' feet,*
*and he will make me to walk upon mine high places.*

**Habakkuk 3:19**

See not the small trials and vexations of each hour of the day. See the purpose and plan to which all are leading. If in climbing a mountain you keep your eyes on each stony or difficult place as you ascend, how weary and profitless your climb!

But if you think of each step as leading to the summit of achievement, then your climb will be so different.

# SUBLIME HEIGHTS

*If it be so, our God whom we serve is able to deliver us from the burning*

*fiery furnace, and he will deliver us out of thine hand, O king.*

### DANIEL 3:17

I am your deliverer. Trust in Me absolutely. I will do the very

best for you.

Know that with Me all things are possible.

Say many times, "All things are possible with my Master,

my Lord, my friend."

This truth, accepted and firmly believed in, is the ladder

up which a soul can climb from the lowest of pits to the

sublimest of heights.

# EXHAUSTION

*Strait is the gate, and narrow is the way, which leadeth unto life,*
*and few there be that find it.*

MATTHEW 7:14

Many wonderful things would not have happened but for the physical weariness, the mind-weariness of My servants, which made the resting apart, the giving up of work, a necessity.

Though My way may seem a narrow way, it yet leads to abundant life. Follow it. It is not so narrow but that I can tread it beside you.

A comrade infinitely tender, infinitely strong, will tread the way with you.

# ACCEPT TRIALS

*In God have I put my trust: I will not be afraid what man can do unto me.*

**PSALM 56:11**

Trials and troubles may seem to overwhelm you. They cannot do more than work My will, and that will you have said is your will.

Do you not see that you cannot be destroyed?

From now a new life is opening out before you. Yours to enter into the kingdom I have prepared for you.

The sunlight of My presence is on your path. Trust and go forward unafraid. My grace is sufficient for all your needs.

# TANGLED SKEINS

*He maketh me to lie down in green pastures: he leadeth me beside the still waters. . . . He leadeth me in the paths of righteousness for his name's sake.*

PSALM 23:2–3

Am I not leading you faithfully?

Directly you put your cares into My hands, and I began to effect a cure of all the disharmony and disorder.

You must know that I shall cause you no more pain in the doing of it than a physician, who knows he can effect a cure, would cause his patient. I will do all as tenderly as possible.

# CONTINUOUS SERVICE

*If any man serve me, let him follow me; and where I am, there shall also*

*my servant be: if any man serve me, him will my Father honour.*

JOHN 12:26

Service is the law of heaven. My angels do always obey. "They serve Him continually" can be said of all who love Me.

With love there is continuous service in every action, and also even in rest.

Take this not as the end but as the beginning of a new life consecrated to My service.

A life of power and joy.

# Breathe My Name

*The name of the Lord is a strong tower:*

*the righteous runneth into it, and is safe.*

## Proverbs 18:10

Just breathe My name.

It is like the pressure of a child's hand that calls forth an answering pressure, which strengthens the child's confidence and banishes fear.

# GIVE, GIVE, GIVE

*Give, and it shall be given unto you; good measure, pressed down, and shaken together, and running over, shall men give into your bosom.*

LUKE 6:38

Give abundantly. Feel that you are rich. Have no mean thought in your heart.

Of love, of thought, of all you have, give, give, give.

You are followers of the world's greatest giver. Give of time, of personal ease and comfort, of rest, of fame, of healing, of power, of sympathy, of all these and many more.

Learn this lesson, and you will become a great power to help others.

# Pray and Deny

*This kind goeth not out but by prayer and fasting.*

**Matthew 17:21**

You must live a life of communion and prayer if you are to save others.

Take My words as a command to you. "By prayer and fasting."

Pray and deny yourself, and you will be used marvelously to save and help others.

# HOW RICH YOU ARE

*I will never leave thee, nor forsake thee.*

### HEBREWS 13:5

My child, that word is unfailingly true. Down the centuries thousands have proved My constancy.

My love, My understanding, My strength will never leave you. Think of all that I am:

Love—then forever you are sure of love.

Strength—then forever, in every difficulty and danger, you are sure of strength.

Patience—then always there is One who can never tire.

Understanding—then always you will be understood.

Can you fear the future when it holds so much for you?

# I MUST PROVIDE

*Thomas answered and said unto him, My LORD and my God.*

JOHN 20:28

I am your Lord. Enough. Then I can command your obedient service, your loyalty. But I am bound by My lordship to give you protection.

I am bound to fight for you, to plan for you, to secure you a sufficiency of all within My power to provide. Think how vast that provision can be. Never doubt.

Such marvels are unfolding. Wonders beyond your dreams. They only need the watering of a grateful spirit and a loving heart to yield abundantly.

# LIVE IN THE UNSEEN

*The spirit of man is the candle of the LORD,*
*searching all the inward parts of the belly.*

### PROVERBS 20:27

You are living in the unseen—that is the real life.

Lift up your head from earth's troubles, and view the glories of the kingdom. Speak to Me. Long for Me. Rest in Me. Abide in Me. No restlessly bringing Me your burdens, then feverishly lifting them again and bearing them away.

No! Abide in Me. Not for one moment losing the consciousness of My strength and protection.

# DROP THOSE BURDENS

*When he had taken the five loaves and the two fishes, he. . .blessed,*

*and brake the loaves. . . . And they that did eat of the loaves*

*were about five thousand men.*

MARK 6:41, 44

Look to Me for all. Rely on Me for all. Drop those burdens, and then, singing and free, you can go on your way rejoicing. Encumbered with them you will fall.

Drop them at My feet, knowing surely that I will lift them and deal with each one as is truly best.

# PROGRESS

*Be not conformed to this world: but be ye transformed by the renewing*

*of your mind, that ye may prove what is that good, and acceptable,*

*and perfect, will of God.*

ROMANS 12:2

Progress is the law of heaven. Higher, ever higher, rise to life
and beauty, knowledge and power.

Tomorrow be stronger, braver, more loving than you
have been today.

The law of progress gives a meaning, a purpose to life.

# YOUR LOVED ONES

*They said, Believe on the Lord Jesus Christ,*

*and thou shalt be saved, and thy house.*

### ACTS 16:31

Your loved ones are very safe in My keeping. Learning and loving and working, theirs is a life of happiness and progress. They live to serve, and serve they truly do. They serve Me and those they love.

You do well to remember your friends in the unseen. Earth's troubles and difficulties will seem, even now, less overwhelming as you look, not at the things that are seen, but at the real, the eternal life.

# Everlasting Arms

*The eternal God is thy refuge, and underneath are the everlasting arms.*

## Deuteronomy 33:27

Arms, sheltering arms, express the loving tenderness of your Father (My Father) in heaven. Man, in his trouble and difficulty, needs nothing so much as a refuge, a place where none and nothing can touch him.

Say to yourself, "He is my refuge." Say it until its truth sinks into your very soul. Say it until you know it—are so sure of it that nothing can make you afraid.

## 8

# WALK IN MY LOVE

*Ye shall walk in all the ways which the LORD your God hath commanded you, that ye may live, and that it may be well with you.*

### DEUTERONOMY 5:33

A consciousness of My presence as love makes all life different. The consciousness of Me means the opening of your whole nature to Me, and that brings relief. Relief brings peace. Peace brings joy.

Beyond all words is My love and care for you. Rejoice in it. Walk in My love. There is a spring in the walk of those who walk in My love.

# CULTIVATE—YOURSELF

*Now thanks be unto God, which always causeth us to triumph in Christ,
and maketh manifest the savour of his knowledge by us in every place.*

## 2 CORINTHIANS 2:14

Bend your knees in wonder before My revelation. The joy of
seeing spiritual truths is a great joy.

Remember your great field of labor is yourself. That
is your first task, the weeding, planting, digging, pruning,
bearing fruit. When that is done I lead you out into other
fields.

*God Calling*

**10**

SEPTEMBER

# GOD OR MAMMON?

*No man can serve two masters: for either he will hate the one,*

*and love the other; or else he will hold to the one, and despise the other.*

*Ye cannot serve God and mammon.*

MATTHEW 6:24

Do you want the full and complete satisfaction that you find in Me, and the satisfaction of the world, too? Then you are trying to serve God and mammon, or if not trying to serve, then claiming the wages of both.

Do not expect love or gratitude or acknowledgment from any. All reward necessary I will give you.

# A Generous Giver

*I am come that they might have life,*

*and that they might have it more abundantly.*

John 10:10

Yes, I, your master, am a generous giver. Abundant life, in overflowing measure, I give to you. The eternal life that pulses through your whole being, that animates your mind and body, too.

A generous, kingly giver. For this I came that man might live in Me. Life it was of which I spoke when I said, "I am the vine, ye are the branches." The life-flow of the vine is in the branches.

# MONEY VALUES

*If therefore thine eye be single, thy whole body shall be full of light.*

### MATTHEW 6:22

The eye of the soul is the will. If your one desire is My kingdom, then truly shall your whole body be full of light. When you are told to seek first the kingdom of God, the first step is to secure that your will is for that kingdom.

Know no values but spiritual values. Only seek material gain when that gain will mean a gain for My kingdom. Get away from money values altogether.

# NO OTHER NAME

*Because of the savour of thy good ointments thy name*

*is as ointment poured forth.*

SONG OF SOLOMON 1:3

My name is the power that turns evil aside, that summons all good to your aid. Spoken in fear, in weakness, in sorrow, in pain, it is an appeal I never fail to answer.

Use My name often. Think of the unending call of "Mother" made by her children. To help, to care, to decide, to appeal. Use My name in that same way.

Use it not only when you need help, but to express love.

# WHEN FAITH FAILS

*Lord, I believe; help thou mine unbelief.*

MARK 9:24

This cry of the human heart is as expressive of human need as it was when uttered to Me while I was on earth. It expresses the soul's progress.

As a soul realizes Me and My power, and knows Me as helper and Savior, that soul believes in Me more and more. At the same time it is more conscious than before of its falling short of absolute trust in Me.

# QUIET STRENGTH

*Stand in awe, and sin not: commune with your*

*own heart upon your bed, and be still.*

## PSALM 4:4

Rest in Me. When tired nature rebels, it is her call for rest.
Rest then until My life-power flows through you.

Have no fear for the future. Be quiet, be still, and in that
very stillness your strength will come and will be maintained.

The world sees strength in action. In My kingdom it
is known that strength lies in quiet. "In quietness and in
confidence shall be your strength."

Rest in Me.

*God Calling*

**16**
SEPTEMBER

# ASSURANCE

*Let us draw near with a true heart in full assurance of faith,*
*having our hearts sprinkled from an evil conscience,*
*and our bodies washed with pure water.*

HEBREWS 10:22

My peace it is that gives quietness and assurance forever. My peace that flows as some calm river through the dry land of life.

Success is the result of work done in peace. Only so can work yield its increase.

Abide in Me, and I in you, so shall you bring forth much fruit. Be calm, assured, at rest. Love, not rush. Peace, not unrest.

I love you.

# FALTERING STEPS

*Blessed be the LORD God of my master Abraham. . .I being in the way,*

*the LORD led me to the house of my master's brethren.*

### GENESIS 24:27

Show us Thy way, O Lord, and let us walk in Thy paths.

You are doing so. This is the way. The way of uncertain future and faltering steps. It is My way.

Put all fear of the future aside. Know that you will be led. Know that you will be shown. I have promised.

*God Calling*

## 18
### SEPTEMBER

# DWELL THERE

*He that dwelleth in the secret place of the most High shall*

*abide under the shadow of the Almighty.*

#### PSALM 91:1

Hidden in a sure place, known only to God and you.

But you must dwell therein. No fitful visit, a real abiding. Make it your home.

Over that home shall My shadow rest, to make it doubly safe, doubly secret.

When fears assail you and cares trouble you, then it is because you have ventured out of that protecting shadow. Then the only thing to do is to creep back into shelter again.

# FULL JOY

*Delight thyself also in the Lord: and he shall give thee*

*the desires of thine heart.*

### PSALM 37:4

Remember that the truths I teach you have all been given to you (as to My disciples of old) with the idea of giving you that overflowing joy.

Search for the joy in life. Hunt for it as for hidden treasure. Delight yourself in the Lord.

Joy in Me. Full joy it was I wished My disciples to have. I intended them to have it.

# TASTE AND TRUST

*O taste and see that the LORD is good.*

PSALM 34:8

He is good. Trust in Him. Know that all is well. Leave in His hands the present and the future, knowing only that He is good. He can bring order out of chaos, good out of evil, peace out of turmoil.

I and My Father are one, one in desire to do good. For God to do good to His children is for Him to share His goodness with them. God is eager to share His goodness with you, and He will do this.

# SEE THE FATHER

*Have I been so long time with you, and yet hast thou not known me, Philip?*

*he that hath seen me hath seen the Father.*

## JOHN 14:9

Have I been so long time with you, coming to you, speaking to you, and yet have you not known the Father?

Your Father is the God and controller of a mighty universe. But He is as I am. All the love and the strength and the beauty you have seen in Me are in My Father.

If you see that, then that is really sufficient for you.

# JOY-TRIBUTE

*Sing unto him a new song; play skilfully with a loud noise.*

*For the word of the LORD is right; and all his works are done in truth.*

PSALM 33:3–4

Sing unto Me from a glad heart. Sing and praise My holy name. Praise is man's joy-tribute to Me, and as you praise, thrills of joy surge through your being, and you learn something of the joy of the heavenly host.

# TURN AGAIN

*Draw nigh to God, and he will draw nigh to you.*

### JAMES 4:8

You must turn to Me before you are conscious of My nearness. It is that turning to Me you must cultivate in every circumstance.

It is so wonderful that naught is needed but that mute appeal. You have no need to voice your longing. No need to plead, no need to bring gifts. How wonderful to feel you can so simply claim help, and so promptly, so lovingly, it is there.

Not only help, but the comfort and joy of divine nearness and companionship.

# LEARN OF ME

*Lord, to whom shall we go? thou hast the words of eternal life.*

JOHN 6:68

Learn of no one but Me. Teachers are to point the way to Me. After that you must accept Me, the great Teacher.

The words of eternal life are all the words controlling your being, even your temporal life. Take these, too, from Me. Have no fear. Abide in Me and accept My ruling.

Be full of gratitude. Wing up your prayers on praise to heaven. Take all that happens as My planning. All is well.

# COME AND STAY

*Let us labour therefore to enter into that rest.*

## HEBREWS 4:11

Yes, come for rest. But stay for rest, too. Stop all feverish haste and be calm and untroubled. Come unto Me, not only for petitions to be granted, but for nearness to Me.

Be sure of My help, be conscious of My presence, and wait until My rest fills your soul.

Rest knows no fear, no want. Rest is strong, sure. Rest, and all you need to gain this rest is to come to Me.

# SERVE ALL

*Whosoever will be chief among you, let him be your servant.*

MATTHEW 20:27

Remember to serve all. Be ready to prove your sonship by service. Look on all you meet as guests in your Father's house, to be treated with love, consideration, and gentleness.

As a servant of all, think no work beneath you. Be ever ready to do all you can for others.

When you serve others, you are acting for your Master and Lord, who washed His disciples' feet. So, in service for others, express your love for Me.

# DIVINE RESTRAINT

*Of the increase of his government and peace there shall be no end.*

ISAIAH 9:7

Think how tenderly I respect the right of each individual soul. Never forcing upon it My help, My salvation. Perhaps in all My suffering for humanity that is the hardest, the restraint of the divine impatience and longing to help, until the call of the soul gives Me My right to act.

Think of love shown in this. Comfort My waiting, loving, longing heart by claiming My help, guidance, and miracle-working power.

# THE SECRET PATH

*Suffer it to be so now: for thus it becometh us to fulfil all righteousness.*

**MATTHEW 3:15**

Beloved, you are called to save and share in a very special way. The way of sorrows, if walked with Me, the Man of Sorrows, is a path kept sacred and secret for My nearest and dearest, those whose one desire is to do all for Me.

But dreary as that path must look to those who view it only from afar, it has tender lights and restful shades that no other walk in life can give.

# I Touch Your Arm

*They. . .besought him that they might only touch the hem of his garment: and as many as touched were made perfectly whole.*

## Matthew 14:35–36

When you look to Me for guidance, My hand is laid upon your arm, a gentle touch to point the way. When in mental, physical, or spiritual weakness you cry to Me for healing, My touch brings strength and healing, the renewal of your youth, the power to climb and strive.

My touch has still its ancient power, and that power is promised to you.

# WISDOM

*Teach us to number our days, that we may apply our hearts unto wisdom.*

PSALM 90:12

"As thy days, so shall thy strength be."

I have promised that for every day you live, the strength shall be given you. Do not fear.

Face each difficulty sure that the wisdom and strength will be given you for it. Claim it.

Rely on Me to keep My promise about this. In My universe, for every task I give one of My children, there is set aside all that is necessary for its performance. So why fear? Why doubt?

# SECRET OF PROSPERITY

*Look unto me, and be ye saved, all the ends of the earth.*

ISAIAH 45:22

Look to no other source for salvation. Look unto Me, and you shall be saved. Regard Me as your only supply. That is the secret of prosperity for you, and you in your turn shall save many from poverty and distress.

Whatever danger threatens, look unto Me. Whatever you desire or need, or desire or need for others, look unto Me. Claim all from My storehouse.

# TRUE MEEKNESS

*I can of mine own self do nothing. . .I seek not mine own will,*
*but the will of the Father which hath sent me.*

JOHN 5:30

How easy it is to lead and guide when you are responsive to My wish! The hurts of life come only when you resist My hand.

But in willing My will, there must be a gladness.

"The meek shall inherit the earth," I said. That is, the meek shall control others and the material forces of the earth.

But this is the result of a yielded will. That was My meaning of the word meek.

# BLESSED ASSURANCE

*The work of righteousness shall be peace; and the effect of righteousness*
*quietness and assurance for ever.*

### ISAIAH 32:17

Be still and know that I am God. Only when the soul attains this calm can true work be done, and mind and soul and body be strong to conquer and to bear.

The peace is the work of righteousness living the right life, living with Me. Quietness and assurance follow.

Assurance is the calm born of a deep certainty in Me, in My promises, in My power to save and keep. Gain this calm.

# ALL YOU DESIRE

*He hath no form nor comeliness; and when we shall see him,*
*there is no beauty that we should desire him.*

ISAIAH 53:2

In this verse My servant Isaiah spoke of the wonderful illumination given to those who were Spirit-guided.

To those who know Me not, there is in Me nothing to attract them.

To those who know Me, there is nothing more to be desired.

Oh! My child, draw very near to Me. See Me as I really am, that ever you may have the joy of finding in Me all you could desire.

# NO CHANCE MEETINGS

*The LORD shall preserve thy going out and thy coming in from this time forth, and even for evermore.*

**PSALM 121:8**

All your movements, your goings and comings, controlled by Me.

Every meeting not a chance meeting, but planned by Me. All blessed.

Led by the Spirit, a proof of sonship. "As many as are led by the Spirit of God, they are the sons of God," and if children, then heirs of God.

What a heritage!

Your suffering has its purpose. It leads to perfection of character and to union with Me.

# A Child's Hand

*Thou hast made thy servant king instead of David my father:*
*and I am but a little child: I know not how to go out or come in.*

1 KINGS 3:7

Do you not know what it means to feel a little trusting hand in yours, to know a child's confidence?

Does that not draw out your love and desire to protect? Think what My heart feels, when in your helplessness you turn to Me.

Would you fail that child, faulty and weak as you are? Could I fail you? Just know it is not possible.

# REJOICE AT WEAKNESS

*Hast thou not heard, that the everlasting God, the L*ORD*, the Creator of the ends of the earth, fainteth not, neither is weary? there is no searching of his understanding.*

ISAIAH 40:28

I know all. Every cry for mercy. Every sigh of weariness. Every plea for help. Every sorrow over failure. Every weakness.

I am with you through all. My tender sympathy is yours. My strength is yours.

Rejoice at your weakness. My strength is made perfect in weakness. When you are weak, then am I strong. Strong to help, to cure, to protect.

# THE DARK PLACES

*As he sat at meat, there came a woman having an alabaster box of ointment of spikenard very precious; and she brake the box, and poured it on his head.*

**MARK 14:3**

Love Me until just to think of Me means joy and rapture. Healing for all physical, mental, and spiritual ills you can always find in thinking of Me.

Are doubts and fears in your heart? Then think of Me, speak to Me. Instead of those fears and doubts, there will flow into your heart such sweet joy as is beyond any joy of earth.

# LOVE ME MORE

*Whom having not seen, ye love; in whom, though now ye see him not,*

*yet believing, ye rejoice with joy unspeakable and full of glory.*

### 1 PETER 1:8

I would draw you closer to Me by bonds of love. The love of the sinner for the Savior, of the rescued for the Rescuer, of the sheep for the loving Shepherd, of the child for his Father. Each experience in your life makes its own particular demand upon Me. Each serves to answer the prayer "Make me love Thee more and more."

# EXTRA WORK

*The Comforter, which is the Holy Ghost. . .shall teach you all things, and bring all things to your remembrance, whatsoever I have said unto you.*

JOHN 14:26

You are My servant. Serve Me as simply, cheerfully, and readily as you expect others to serve you.

Do you blame the servant who avoids extra work? Do you feel you are ill served by such a one?

Then what of Me? Is not that how you so often serve Me? Lay this to heart and view your day's work in this light.

# SHAME AND DISTRESS

*I will bless the LORD at all times: his praise shall continually be*

*in my mouth. . . . I sought the LORD, and he heard me,*

*and delivered me from all my fears.*

**PSALM 34:1, 4**

Before you cry in your distress, bless the Lord, even when
troubles seem to overwhelm you.

I will do My part, and deliverance will be sure.

The shame and distress will be lifted, too. First right with
Me, and then you will be righted, too, in the eyes of men.

# You Are My Joy

*Thine they were, and thou gavest them me; and they have kept thy word.*

### John 17:6

Just as you thank God for Me, so I thank God for His gift to Me of you. In that hour of My agony on earth, one note of joy thrilled through the pain. The thought of the souls who had kept My word.

They had not yet done great deeds for, and in, My name. They were simple doers of My word.

You, too, can bring joy to My heart by faithful service in the little things.

# THE SCULPTOR'S SKILL

*Then touched he their eyes, saying, According to your faith be it unto you.*

### MATTHEW 9:29

No misspent time over failures and shortcomings. Count the lessons learned from them as rungs in the ladder.

Learn another lesson. The sculptor who finds a faulty marble casts it aside. Because it has no fashioning, it may regard itself as perfect; and it may look with scorn upon the marble the sculptor is cutting and shaping into perfection. From this learn a lesson for your life.

# THE SACRIFICE

*Behold the Lamb of God, which taketh away the sin of the world.*

**JOHN 1:29**

Christ our Passover is sacrificed for us. I am the Lamb of God. Lay upon Me your sins, your failures, your shortcomings. My sacrifice has atoned for all. I am the mediator between God and man, the man Christ Jesus.

Do not dwell upon the past. You make My sacrifice of no effect.

No! Realize that in Me you have all, complete forgiveness, complete companionship, complete healing.

# FEEL PLENTY

*Every beast of the forest is mine, and the cattle upon a thousand hills. . . .*

*If I were hungry, I would not tell thee: for the world is mine,*

*and the fulness thereof.*

PSALM 50:10, 12

Live in My secret place, and there the feeling is one of full satisfaction. You are to feel plenty. The storehouses of God are full to overflowing.

Think thoughts of plenty. See yourselves as children of a king. Wish plenty for yourselves and all you care for and long to help.

# THE IMPRISONED GOD

*Trust in the LORD, and do good.*

**PSALM 37:3**

However little you may be able to remedy financial affairs, you can always turn to yourselves and, seeing something not in order there, seek to right that.

As all reform is from within out, you will always find the outward has improved, too. To do this is to release the imprisoned God–power within you.

That power, once operative, will immediately perform miracles.

# Faith-Vision

*Looking unto Jesus. . .who for the joy that was set before him endured the cross. . .and is set down at the right hand of the throne of God.*

**Hebrews 12:2**

Turn your eyes to behold Me. Look away from sordid surroundings, from the imperfections in yourselves and those around you. Then you who have the faith-vision will see all you could and do desire in Me.

In your unrest, behold My calm. In your impatience, My unfailing patience. In your lack and limitation, My perfection.

Looking at Me, you will grow like Me.

# LONELINESS

*And they all forsook him, and fled.*

**MARK 14:50**

I know what loneliness, desertion, and solitude mean. Every act of yours of faithfulness is a comfort to My heart. It was to those deserters I gave the task of bringing My message to mankind. To those deserters, those fearful ones, I gave My power to heal, to raise to life.

Earth's successes are not the ones I use for the great work of My kingdom. Learn My tender understanding and pardon of human frailty. Not until man has failed has he learned true humility.

# HEAR MY ANSWER

*If we ask any thing according to his will, he heareth us: and if we know*

*that he hear us, whatsoever we ask, we know that we have the petitions*

*that we desired of him.*

## 1 JOHN 5:14–15

The cry of the human soul is never unheard. It is never that God does not hear the cry, but that man fails to hear the response.

But man treats this cry as if it were a thing alone, not realizing that the response was there in all eternity, and only man's failing to listen kept him unhelped by it.

# No Burden Irks

*Walk as children of light: (for the fruit of the Spirit is in all goodness and righteousness and truth;) proving what is acceptable unto the Lord.*

### Ephesians 5:8–10

Simple acceptance of My will is the key to divine revelation. It will result in both holiness and happiness. The way to the cross may be a way of sorrow, but at its foot the burdens of sin and earth-desire are rolled away.

The yoke of acceptance of My Father's will in all things is adjusted to My servants' shoulders, and from that moment no burden irks.

# A LOVE FEAST

*Behold, I stand at the door, and knock: if any man hear my voice, and open the door, I will come in to him, and will sup with him, and he with me.*

## REVELATION 3:20

You think it would have been joy to have been at the marriage feast of Cana of Galilee, or to have been one of My disciples seated with Me at the Last Supper!

But at each of these feasts you could not have known the rapture you may know as you hear the knocking and, opening, bid Me welcome to My feast.

# HOME-BUILDING

*But ye, beloved, building up yourselves on your most holy faith,*
*praying in the Holy Ghost.*

JUDE 1:20

You are building up an unshakable faith. Be furnishing the quiet places of your souls now.

Fill them with all that is harmonious, good, beautiful, and enduring.

Home-build in the Spirit now, and the waiting time will be well spent.

# HILL OF SACRIFICE

*Ye shall be hated of all men for my name's sake:*

*but he that endureth to the end shall be saved.*

MATTHEW 10:22

You must trust to the end.

You must know even when you cannot see. You must
be ready, like My servant Abraham, to climb the very hill of
sacrifice, to go to the very last moment, before you see My
deliverance.

This final test has to come to all who walk by faith. You
must rely on Me alone.

Look to no other arm; look for no other help.

# SALT OF THE EARTH

*Ye are the salt of the earth: but if the salt have lost his savour. . .*

*it is thenceforth good for nothing, but to be cast out,*

*and to be trodden under foot of men.*

**MATTHEW 5:13**

There is the keeping that I ensure to those of whom I speak as the salt of the earth.

Only in very close contact with Me is the keeping power realized. That keeping power that maintains the salt at its freshest and best, and also preserves from corruption that portion of the world in which I place it.

# No Unemployment

*They overcame him by the blood of the Lamb, and by the word of their*

*testimony; and they loved not their lives unto the death.*

### Revelation 12:11

The way of conquest over the temporal is learned by the conquest of the self-life.

Seek daily more and more to obtain this self-conquest, and you are gaining surely, though you may not see it, conquest over the temporal forces and powers.

Unemployment would cease if man realized this.

# DESERTERS

*Yea, mine own familiar friend, in whom I trusted, which did eat of my*

*bread, hath lifted up his heel against me.*

PSALM 41:9

You must believe utterly. My love can bear nothing less. I am so often "wounded in the house of My friends." Do you think the spitting and scorn of My enemies hurt me? No!

It is not the unbelief of My enemies that hurts, but that My friends, who love and know Me, cannot walk all the way with Me, and doubt My power to do all that I have said.

# DAYS OF CONQUEST

*Thanks be to God, which giveth us the victory*
*through our Lord Jesus Christ.*

1 CORINTHIANS 15:57

I see the loving, striving, not the defects. I see the conquest
of your particular battle. I count it victory, a glad victory.
I do not compare it with the strenuous campaigns of My
great saints.

For you it is victory, and the angels rejoice, and your dear
ones rejoice, as much as at any conquest noted and rejoiced
over by heaven.

Count the days of conquest as very blessed days.

# GLAD SURPRISES

*Do all things without murmurings and disputings.*

**PHILIPPIANS 2:14**

Bow to My will not as one who is resigned to some heavy blow about to fall or to the acceptance of some inevitable decision.

Bow as a child bows, in anticipation of a glad surprise being prepared for him by one who loves him.

Bow in such a way, just waiting to hear the loving word to raise your head and see the glory and joy and wonder of your surprise.

# DISCOUNT MONEY

*Let this mind be in you, which was also in Christ Jesus.*

## PHILIPPIANS 2:5

Never count success by money gained. That is not the mind of My kingdom. Your success is the measure of My will and mind that you have revealed to those around you.

Your success is the measure of My will that those around you have seen worked out in your life.

# THE HARDEST LESSON

*Our soul waiteth for the LORD: he is our help and our shield.*

**PSALM 33:20**

Wait, and you shall realize the joy of the one who can be calm and wait, knowing that all is well. The last and hardest lesson is that of waiting.

I would almost say tonight, "Forgive Me that I allow this extra burden to rest upon you even for so short a time."

Use this waiting time to cement your friendship with Me and to increase your knowledge of Me.

# THE VOICE AGAIN

*Thy word is a lamp unto my feet, and a light unto my path.*

## PSALM 119:105

My Word, the Scriptures. Read them; study them; store them in your heart.

But remember, My word is more even than that. It is the voice that speaks to your heart.

It is the voice that speaks to you intimately. It is even more than that. It is I, your Lord and friend.

"And the Word was made flesh, and dwelt among us." Truly a lamp to your feet and a light to your path.

# PRAYER OF JOY

*Another angel came. . .having a golden censer. . . .*
*And the smoke of the incense, which came with the prayers of the saints,*
*ascended up before God out of the angel's hand.*

REVELATION 8:3–4

Prayer can be like incense, rising ever higher and higher, or it can be like a low earth-mist clinging to the ground, never once soaring.

The prayer of real faith is the prayer of joy, which sees and knows the heart of love it rises to greet, and which is so sure of a glad response.

# SPEND

*For the love of money is the root of all evil.*

1 TIMOTHY 6:10

Give, give, give. Keep ever an empty vessel for Me to fill. In future use all for Me, and give all you cannot use.

How poor die those who leave wealth! Wealth is to use, to spend, for Me.

Use as you go. Delight to use.

# NO LIMIT

*Ye ask, and receive not, because ye ask amiss,*

*that ye may consume it upon your lusts.*

JAMES 4:3

Unlimited supply, that is My law. Will you feel this, that there is no limit to My power?

But man asks such poor, mean things. I desire to give you a gift, and if you are content with the poor, the mean, and the sordid, then you are insulting Me, the giver.

"Ask what ye will, and it shall be done unto you." Have a big faith, and expect big things, and you will get big things.

# I Am Beside You

*In thy presence is fulness of joy; at thy right hand there*
*are pleasures for evermore.*

**PSALM 16:11**

Do not seek to realize this fullness of joy as the result of
effort. This cannot be, any more than joy in a human friend's
presence would come as the result of trying to force yourself
to like having that friend with you.

Call often My name.

The calling of My name does not really summon Me.
I am beside you. But it removes, as it were, the scales from
your eyes, and you see Me.

# Second Advent

*He must increase, but I must decrease.*

JOHN 3:30

The world would be brought to Me so soon if only all who acknowledge Me as Lord gave themselves unreservedly to be used by Me.

I do not delay My second coming. My followers delay it.

If each lived for Me, by Me, in Me, allowing Me to live in him, to use him to express the divine through him, then long ago the world would have been drawn to Me, and I should have come to claim My own.

# GOD IN ACTION

*Because he loved thy fathers, therefore he chose their seed after them,*

*and brought thee out in his sight with his mighty power out of Egypt.*

DEUTERONOMY 4:37

Power is just God in action.

Therefore whenever a servant of Mine, however weak he humanly may be, allows God to work through him, all he does is powerful.

Carry this thought with you through the days in which you seem to accomplish little. Try to see it is not you, but the divine Spirit in you. All you have to do is to turn self out.

# SELF KILLS POWER

*Grieve not the holy Spirit of God,*

*whereby ye are sealed unto the day of redemption.*

### EPHESIANS 4:30

When you dwell with Me, desiring only My will and to do My work, My Spirit cannot fail to pass through the channel of your life into the lives of others.

The only block there can be in your channel is self. Keep that out, and know that My Spirit is flowing through. Therefore all must be the better for coming in contact with you.

# WIPE THE SLATE

*Jesus said unto him, No man, having put his hand to the plough,*
*and looking back, is fit for the kingdom of God.*

LUKE 9:62

Forget the past. Remember only its glad days. Wipe the slate of your remembrance with love, which will erase all that is not confirmed in love. You must forget your failures and those of others. Wipe them out of the book of your remembrance.

If you forget not the sins of others, and I bear them, then you add to My sorrows.

# WONDERFUL FRIENDSHIP

*Ye are my friends, if ye do whatsoever I command you.*

## JOHN 15:14

Think of Me as a friend, but realize, too, the wonder of the friendship. As soon as man gives Me not only worship and honor, obedience and allegiance, but loving understanding, then he becomes My friend, even as I am his.

What I can do for you. Yes! But also what we can do for each other. What you can do for Me.

Your service becomes so different when you feel I count on your great friendship to do this or that for Me.

# New Forces

*This poor man cried, and the LORD heard him,*
*and saved him out of all his troubles.*

PSALM 34:6

Life's difficulties and troubles are intended not to arrest your progress, but to increase your speed. You must call new forces into action.

Whatever it is that must be surmounted, overcome.

It is as a race. Nothing must daunt you. Do not let a difficulty conquer you. You must conquer it.

My strength will be there awaiting you. Nothing is too small to be faced and overcome. To push small difficulties aside is to be preparing big troubles.

# HEAVEN'S COLORS

*When thou goest, thy steps shall not be straitened;*
*and when thou runnest, thou shalt not stumble.*

PROVERBS 4:12

Looking back you will see that every step was planned. Leave all to Me. Each stone in the mosaic fits into the perfect pattern, designed by the master artist.

It is all so wonderful!

But the colors are of heaven's hues, so that your eyes could not bear to gaze on the whole until you are beyond the veil.

So stone by stone you see, and trust the pattern to the designer.

# DEVIOUS WAYS

*I will bring the blind by a way that they knew not; I will lead them in paths that they have not known: I will make darkness light before them, and crooked things straight.*

ISAIAH 42:16

Life is not easy, My child. Man has made of it not what My Father meant it to be.

Ways that were meant to be straight paths have been made by man into ways devious and evil, filled with obstacles and stones of difficulty.

# By My Spirit

*They went forth, and preached every where, the Lord working with them, and confirming the word with signs following.*

**MARK 16:20**

Man is apt to think that once in time only was My miracle-working power in action. That is not so. Wherever man trusts wholly in Me, and leaves to Me the choosing of the very day and hour, then there is My miracle-working power as manifest as ever it was when I was on earth.

Trust in Me. "Not by might, nor by power, but by My Spirit, saith the Lord."

# UNION IS POWER

*Where two or three are gathered together in my name,*

*there am I in the midst of them.*

**MATTHEW 18:20**

Claim that promise always. When two of My lovers meet, I am the third. Never limit that promise.

When you two are together in My name, united by one bond in My Spirit, I am there. Not only when you meet to greet Me and to hear My voice.

Think what this means in power. It is again the lesson of the power that follows two united to serve Me.

# QUIET LIVES

*Well done, thou good and faithful servant. . .*

*enter thou into the joy of thy lord.*

MATTHEW 25:21

These words are whispered in the ears of many whom the world would pass by. Not to the great and the world-famed are these words said so often, but to the quiet followers who serve Me unobtrusively, yet faithfully, who bear their cross bravely, with a smiling face to the world. Thank Me for the quiet lives.

The world may never see the humble, patient, quiet service, but I see it, and My reward is joy divine.

# DAZZLING GLORY

*Arise, shine; for thy light is come,*

*and the glory of the LORD is risen upon thee.*

**ISAIAH 60:1**

The glory of the Lord is the beauty of His character.

The beauty of the purity and love of God is too dazzling for mortals to see in full.

The glory of the Lord is risen upon you when you reflect that glory in your lives, when in love, patience, service, purity, whatever it may be, you reveal to the world something of the Father, an assurance that you have been with Me.

# HILLS OF THE LORD

*I will lift up mine eyes unto the hills, from whence cometh my help.*

*My help cometh from the LORD, which made heaven and earth.*

**PSALM 121:1–2**

Raise your eyes from earth's sordid and mean and false, to the hills of the Lord. From poverty, lift your eyes to the help of the Lord.

In moments of weakness, lift your eyes to the hills of the Lord.

For all your spiritual needs, look to the Lord, who made heaven, and for all your temporal needs, look to Me, owner of all this, the Lord who made the earth.

# MYSTERIES

*Why art thou cast down, O my soul? and why art thou disquieted*

*within me? hope in God: for I shall yet praise him,*

*who is the health of my countenance, and my God.*

PSALM 43:5

Do not try to find answers to the mysteries of the world.
Learn to know Me more, and in that knowledge you will have
all the answers you need here.

I was the answer in time to all man's questions about My
Father and His laws. Know no theology. Know Me. All you
need to know about God you know in Me.

# RADIATE JOY

*Let your light so shine before men, that they may see your good works,*

*and glorify your Father which is in heaven.*

MATTHEW 5:16

Not only must you rejoice, but your joy must be made manifest. A candle must be set not under a bushel, but on a candlestick, that it may give light to all who are in the house. Men must see and know your joy and, seeing it, know without any doubt that it springs from living with Me.

The hard, dull way of resignation is not My way.

# ONLY LOVE LASTS

*Though I speak with the tongues of men and of angels, and have not charity,*

*I am become as sounding brass, or a tinkling cymbal.*

## 1 Corinthians 13:1

Only what is done in love lasts, for God is love, and only the work of God remains.

The fame of the world, the applause given to the one who speaks with the tongues of men and of angels, who attracts admiration and compels attention, it is all given to what is really worthless if it lacks that God-quality, love.

# EARTH'S FURIES

*In the world ye shall have tribulation: but be of good cheer;*

*I have overcome the world.*

JOHN 16:33

Then you may ask why you must have tribulation if I have overcome the world.

My overcoming was never for Myself, but for you.

The powers of evil were strained to their utmost to devise means to break Me. They failed, but how they failed was known only to Me and My Father. Reviled, spat upon, scourged—the world, even My own followers, would deem Me conquered. How could they know My Spirit was free, unbroken, unharmed?

# SUFFER TO SAVE

*Whatsoever ye do, do it heartily, as to the Lord, and not unto men;*
*knowing that of the Lord ye shall receive the reward of the inheritance:*
*for ye serve the Lord Christ.*

COLOSSIANS 3:23–24

Take each day's happenings as work you can do for Me. In that spirit a blessing will attend all you do. Offering your day's service thus to Me, you are sharing in My lifework and therefore helping Me to save My world.

The power of vicarious sacrifice is redemptive beyond man's power of understanding here on earth.

# The Heavenly Beggar

*But [Christ Jesus] made himself of no reputation,*

*and took upon him the form of a servant.*

## Philippians 2:7

To those who do not feel their need of Me, who shut the doors of their hearts so that I may not enter, to these I go in tender, humble longing. Even when I find all closed, I stand a beggar, knocking. The heavenly Beggar in His great humility.

Never think of those who have shut you out or forgotten you, that now you have no need of them. No! Remember the heavenly Beggar and learn of Me humility.

# MY BEAUTY

*The LORD God, merciful and gracious, longsuffering,*
*and abundant in goodness and truth. . .*

EXODUS 34:6

The God who was to be born upon earth was not to be housed in a body so beautiful that men would adore Him for the beauty of His countenance.

Pray for the eye to see the beauty of My character. Pray for faith to see the beauty of My love in My dealings with you.

# Not Thwarted

*Saying, Father, if thou be willing, remove this cup from me:*
*nevertheless not my will, but thine, be done.*

LUKE 22:42

I want no will laid grudgingly upon My altar. I want you to desire and love My will, because therein lies your happiness and spirit-rest.

Whenever you feel that you cannot leave the choice to Me, then pray, not to be able to accept My will, but to know and love Me more. With that knowledge, and the love, will come the certainty that I want only the best for you and yours.

# THE WAY OF THE SPIRIT

*Then we which are alive and remain shall be caught up together with*

*them in the clouds, to meet the Lord in the air.*

1 THESSALONIANS 4:17

To work from a desire for great activities to the inner-circle life with Me is really the wrong way. That is why so often when a soul finds Me, I have to begin our friendship by cutting away the ties that bind it to the outer circle. When it has learned its lesson in the inner circle, it can then widen its life.

This is the way of the Spirit.

# WHEN TWO AGREE

*Not forsaking the assembling of ourselves together, as the manner of some is;*

*but exhorting one another: and so much the more,*

*as ye see the day approaching.*

### HEBREWS 10:25

Every promise of Mine shall be fulfilled.

First, "gathered together in My name," bound by a common loyalty to Me, desirous only of doing My will.

Then, when this is so, I am present, too, and when I am there and one with you, voicing the same petition, making your demands Mine, then it follows the request is granted.

# From Self to God

*Thou hast been a shelter for me.*

**Psalm 61:3**

A place to flee to, a sanctuary. An escape from misunderstanding, from yourself. You can get away from others into the quiet of your own being, but from yourself, from the sense of your failure, your weakness, your sins and shortcomings, whither can you flee?

To the eternal God your refuge. Till in His immensity you forget your smallness, meanness, limitations.

Till the relief of safety merges into joy of appreciation of your refuge, and you absorb the divine, and absorbing gain strength to conquer.

# RESPONSIBILITY

*If a brother or sister be naked, and destitute of daily food,*
*and one of you say unto them, Depart in peace, be ye warmed and filled;*
*notwithstanding ye give them not those things*
*which are needful to the body; what doth it profit?*

JAMES 2:15–16

"Lord, send them away that they may go into the villages and buy themselves victuals," said My disciples, with no sympathy for the fainting, exhausted men, women, and children.

But I taught that divine sympathy includes responsibility. "Give ye them to eat," was My reply. I taught that pity, without a remedy for the need, is worthless.

# THE IDEAL MAN

*He hath made him to be sin for us, who knew no sin;*

*that we might be made the righteousness of God in him.*

2 CORINTHIANS 5:21

You speak of your fellow man as falling short of the ideal you had of him. But what of Me? For every man there is the ideal man I see in him.

Judge of My heart when he fails to fulfill that promise. The disappointments of man may be great and many, but they are nothing as compared with My disappointments. Remember this, and strive to be the friend I see in My vision of you.

# A Journey with Me

*The path of the just is as the shining light,*
*that shineth more and more unto the perfect day.*

PROVERBS 4:18

Remember, "I have yet many things to say unto you, but ye cannot bear them now." Only step by step can you proceed in your journey upward.

The one thing to be sure of is that it is a journey with Me. There does come a joy known to those who suffer with Me. But that is not the result of the suffering, but the result of the close intimacy with Me.

# MAN OF SORROWS

*He is despised and rejected of men; a man of sorrows,*

*and acquainted with grief: and we hid as it were our faces from him;*

*he was despised, and we esteemed him not.*

ISAIAH 53:3

My disciples must ever seek to set aside the valuation of the world and judge only according to the values of heaven. Do not seek the praise of men.

When human help fails, keep very close to the Man of Sorrows. Feel My hand of love press yours in silent but complete understanding. No heart can ache without My heart aching, too.

# LAW OF SUPPLY

*Give to him that asketh thee, and from him that would borrow*

*of thee turn not thou away.*

MATTHEW 5:42

The first law of giving is of the spirit-world. Give to all you

meet of your prayers, your time, yourself, your love, your

thought.

Then give of this world's goods, as you have them given

to you. To give money and material things, without having first

made the habit of giving on the higher plane, is wrong.

As you receive, you must supply the needs of those I bring to you.

# EXPECT TEMPTATION

*Lead us not into temptation, but deliver us from evil:*
*For thine is the kingdom, and the power, and the glory, for ever.*

MATTHEW 6:13

The very first step toward conquering temptation is to see it as temptation.

Not to think of it as resulting from your tiredness or illness or poverty, but to realize fully that when you have heard My voice and are going to fulfill your mission to work for Me, you must expect a mighty onslaught from the evil one.

Then for very love of Me you will conquer.

# FOOD OF LIFE

*I have meat to eat that ye know not of.*

JOHN 4:32

Those were My words to My disciples in the early days of My ministry.

Meat is to sustain the body. To do the will of God is the very strength and support of life.

Soul-starvation comes from the failing to do, and to delight in doing, My will. How busy the world is in talking of bodies that are undernourished! What of the souls that are undernourished?

Make it indeed your meat to do My will.

# MY KINGDOM

*Greater works than these shall [ye] do; because I go unto my Father.*

JOHN 14:12

While I was on the earth, to those with whom I came in contact, Mine was a lost cause.

In spite of all I had taught My disciples, they had secretly felt sure that when the final moment came, I should sound some call to action and found My earthly kingdom.

But with My resurrection came hope. Faith revived. They would have the assurance of My divinity. And they would have all My power—the Holy Spirit—to help them.

# YOUR SEARCH REWARDED

*Whom seek ye? And they said, Jesus of Nazareth. Jesus answered,*

*I have told you that I am he.*

JOHN 18:7–8

All men seek for Me, but all men do not know what they want. They are seeking because they are dissatisfied without realizing that I am the object of their quest.

Count it your greatest joy to be the means, by your life, sufferings, words, and love, to prove to the questing ones you know that their search would end when they saw Me.

# THE QUIET TIME

*My beloved spake, and said unto me, Rise up, my love, my fair one,*
*and come away.*

### SONG OF SOLOMON 2:10

There may be many times when I reveal nothing, command nothing, give no guidance. But your path is clear, to grow daily more and more into the knowledge of Me.

I may ask you to sit silent before Me, and I may speak no word that you could write. All the same, waiting with Me will bring comfort and peace. Only friends who understand and love each other can wait silent in each other's presence.

# A SUNRISE GIFT

*This is the day which the LORD hath made; we will rejoice and be glad in it.*

**PSALM 118:24**

To those of My followers whose lives have been full of struggle and care, who have felt the pity of an agonized heart for My poor world—to those I give the peace and joy that bring to age the youth they sacrificed for Me and My world. Take each day now as a joyous sunrise gift from Me. Your simple daily tasks done in My strength and love will bring the consciousness of all your highest hopes.

# CAREFREE

*Perfect love casteth out fear.*

1 JOHN 4:18

Love and fear cannot dwell together. By their very natures they cannot exist side by side. Evil is powerful, and fear is one of evil's most potent forces.

Therefore a weak, vacillating love can be soon routed by fear, whereas a perfect, trusting love is immediately the conqueror, and fear flees in confusion.

The only way to obtain this perfect love that dispels fear is to have Me more and more in your life. You can only banish fear by My presence and My name.

# PERPETUAL GUIDANCE

*That which we have seen and heard declare we unto you,*

*that ye also may have fellowship with us: and truly our fellowship*

*is with the Father, and with his Son.*

### 1 JOHN 1:3

The joy of perpetual guidance, of knowing that every detail of your life is planned by Me with tenderness and love.

Wait for guidance in every step. The thought of this loving leading should give you great joy. All the responsibility of life taken off your shoulders. All its business worry taken off your shoulders.

# STORMS

*Except the LORD build the house, they labour in vain that build it:*
*except the LORD keep the city, the watchman waketh but in vain.*

**PSALM 127:1**

There is no miracle so wonderful as the miracle of a soul kept by My power.

It is like a cool garden set in the midst of a roaring city. Try to see your life as that.

Not only as calm, but as breathing fragrance, expressing beauty. Expect storms. You cannot be united in your great friendship to do My work, and not excite the hatred of all you meet who are not on My side.

# MY SHADOW

*They should seek the Lord. . .for in him we live, and move,*

*and have our being.*

ACTS 17:27–28

Each day must be lived in the consciousness of My presence, even if the thrill of joy seems to be absent. If sometimes there seems a shadow on your life, it is not the withdrawal of My presence. It is My shadow as I stand between you and your foes.

The quiet gray days are the days for duty. Work in the calm certainty that I am with you.

# WHAT JOY IS

*Now the God of hope fill you with all joy and peace in believing,*

*that ye may abound in hope.*

## ROMANS 15:13

Life now for you is a toilsome march. The joy will come, but for the moment do not think of that.

Joy is the reward of patiently seeing Me in the dull, dark days.

Stop thinking your life is all wrong if you do not feel it. You may not yet be joyous, but you are brave, and courage and unselfish thought for others are as sure signs of true discipleship as joy.

# CONDITIONS OF BLESSING

*[The Father] maketh his sun to rise on the evil and on the good,*
*and sendeth rain on the just and on the unjust.*

**MATTHEW 5:45**

When I said this, you will notice it was of material blessings
I spoke.

I did not mean that believer and unbeliever could be
treated alike. I can send rain and sunshine and worldly
blessings equally to both, but of the blessing of the kingdom
that would be impossible.

To attempt to bestow your love on all alike would be
impossible. But temporal blessings you, too, bestow, as does
My Father.

# SEE WONDERS

*Out of the abundance of the heart the mouth speaketh.*

*A good man. . .bringeth forth good things: and an evil man. . .*

*bringeth forth evil things.*

MATTHEW 12:34–35

See wonders, ask wonders, bear wonders away with you.
Remember this beautiful earth on which you are was once
only a thought of divine mind. Think how from your thought
one corner of it could grow and become a garden of the Lord,
a place to which I have a right to bring My friends, My needy
ones, for talk and rest with Me.

# PERFECT LOVE

*Be sober, be vigilant; because your adversary the devil, as a roaring lion,*

*walketh about, seeking whom he may devour:*

*whom resist stedfast in the faith.*

1 PETER 5:8–9

Never fear anybody or anything. No fear that your faith will fail you. No fear of poverty or loneliness. No fear of others. But this absolute casting out of fear is the result of a perfect love of Me. Speak to Me about everything. Listen to Me at all times. Feel My tender nearness, substituting at once some thought of Me for the fear.

# DEPRESSION

*Hear my voice, O God, in my prayer:*
*preserve my life from fear of the enemy.*

PSALM 64:1

Fight fear as you would fight a plague. Fight it in My name. Even the smallest fear is the hacking at the cords of love that bind you to Me.

However small the impression, in time those cords will wear thin, and then one disappointment, or shock, and they snap. But for the little fears, the cords of love would have held.

Depression is a state of fear. Depression is the impression left by fear. Fight and conquer.

# SMILE INDULGENTLY

*He said unto him, Well, thou good servant: because thou hast been*
*faithful in a very little, have thou authority over ten cities.*

LUKE 19:17

Take every moment as of My planning. In all the small things, yield to My gentle pressure on your arm. Stay or go as that pressure indicates.

And when things do not fall out according to your plan, then smile at Me indulgently and say, "Have Your way then"—knowing that My loving response will be to make that way as easy for your feet as it can be.

# Practice Protection

*Yea, though I walk through the valley of the shadow of death, I will fear*
*no evil: for thou art with me; thy rod and thy staff they comfort me.*

### Psalm 23:4

Fear no evil because I have conquered evil.

All you have to do is to say with assurance that whatever it is
cannot harm you. In not only the big but the little things of life,
be sure of My conquering power. Know that all is well. Practice
this. Learn it until it is unfailing and instinctive with you.

# THE WORLD'S SONG

*Let the peace of God rule in your hearts, to the which*
*also ye are called. . .and be ye thankful.*

COLOSSIANS 3:15

Walk with Me in the way of peace. But it must be My peace. Never a peace that is a truce with the power of evil. Never harmony if that means your life-music being adapted to the mood and music of the world.

My disciples so often make the mistake of thinking all must be harmonious. No! Not when it means singing the song of the world.

# HE IS COMING

*The Word was made flesh, and dwelt among us, (and we beheld his glory, the glory as of the only begotten of the Father,) full of grace and truth.*

JOHN 1:14

Remember the first hail must be that of the Magi in the Bethlehem stable, as among the lowliest, bereft of earth's pomp like the Magi.

Then the worship of repentance. As earth's sinner, you stand by Me in the Jordan, baptized of John, worshiping Me, the friend and servant of sinners.

Dwell much on My life.

# BABE OF BETHLEHEM

*Though the LORD be high, yet hath he respect unto the lowly:*

*but the proud he knoweth afar off.*

PSALM 138:6

Kneel before the Babe of Bethlehem. Accept the truth that the kingdom of heaven is for the lowly, the simple.

Bring to Me, the Christ-child, your gifts, truly the gifts of earth's wisest.

The gold—your money.

Frankincense—the adoration of a consecrated life.

Myrrh—your sharing in My sorrows and those of the world.

# HEALTH AND WEALTH

*Trust not in oppression, and become not vain in robbery:*

*if riches increase, set not your heart upon them.*

PSALM 62:10

Health and wealth are coming to you. My wealth, which is sufficiency for your needs and for My work you long to do. Money to hoard is not for My disciples.

Simply seek the means to do My will and work. Never keep anything you are not using. All I give you will be Mine, only given to you to use. Could you think of Me hoarding My treasures? You must never do it.

# Glorious Work

*Riches profit not in the day of wrath:*
*but righteousness delivereth from death.*

**Proverbs 11:4**

I have stripped you of much, that it should be truly a life of well-being. Build up stone by stone upon a firm foundation, and that rock is your master—that rock is Christ.

A life of discipline and joyous fulfillment is to be yours. Never lose sight of the glorious work to which you have been called.

Let no riches, no ease, entice you from the path of miracle-working with Me upon which your feet are set.

# Signs and Feelings

*Thou art near, O Lord; and all thy commandments are truth.*

**Psalm 119:151**

I am here. Do not need feeling too much.

What does it matter what you feel? What matters is what I am, was, and ever shall be to you—a risen Lord. The feeling that I am with you may depend upon any passing mood of yours—upon a change of circumstances, upon a mere trifle.

I am uninfluenced by circumstances. My promise given is kept. I am here, one with you in tender loving friendship.

# WORK AND PRAYER

*The effectual fervent prayer of a righteous man availeth much.*

JAMES 5:16

Work and prayer represent the two forces that will ensure you success. Your work and My work.

For prayer, believing prayer, is based on the certainty that I am working for you and with you and in you.

Go forward gladly and unafraid. I am with you. With men your task may be impossible, but with God all things are possible.

# FISHERS OF MEN

*Say not ye, There are yet four months, and then cometh harvest?*

*behold, I say unto you, Lift up your eyes, and look on the fields;*

*for they are white already to harvest.*

JOHN 4:35

When you think of those who are in anguish, do you ever think how My heart must ache with the anguish of it?

If I beheld the city and wept over it, how much more should I weep over lives that seek to live without My sustaining power.

Live to bring others to Me, the only source of happiness and heart-peace.

# JESUS THE CONQUEROR

*Let them praise the name of the LORD: for his name alone is excellent;*

*his glory is above the earth and heaven.*

**PSALM 148:13**

Jesus. That is the name by which you conquer. "Thou shalt call His name Jesus: for He shall save His people from their sins."

In that word "sins," read not only vice and degradation, but doubts, fears, tempers, despondencies, impatience, lack of love. The very uttering of the name lifts the soul away from petty valley-irritations to mountain heights.

Savior and friend, joy-bringer and rescuer, leader and guide.

Jesus. Say it often.

# SCRIPTURE INDEX

5:16 – November 21

5:42 – December 5

5:44 – April 25

5:45 – December 17

6:6 – January 23

6:8 – November 13

6:11 – February 20

6:13 – December 6

6:22 – September 12

6:24 – September 10

6:33 – March 12

6:34 – April 6

7:1 – May 13

7:7 – April 12

7:14 – August 25

8:26 – July 17

9:21 – February 27

9:29 – October 13

10:19 – April 26

10:22 – October 23

10:42 – May 6

11:28 – January 4

11:29–30 – June 21

12:34-35 – December 18

13:44 – June 30

14:31 – May 12

14:35-36 – September 29

17:20 – May 25

17:21 – August 31

18:2-3 – July 2

18:19 – May 11

18:20 – November 16

20:27 – September 26

25:21 – November 17

26:39 – August 10

28:18 – January 15

## MARK

1:35 – February 28

4:19 – May 21

5:36 – February 3

6:31 – June 23

6:41, 44 – September 4

8:7-9 – March 9

9:24 – September 14

11:24 – May 22

14:3 – October 8

14:50 – October 18

16:20 – November 15

## LUKE

4:18 – May 15

6:38 – August 30

9:23 – March 4

9:62 – November 8

10:39, 42 – February 18

11:1 – June 18

11:9 – April 29

14:33 – April 11

15:6 – April 28

17:6 – February 26

18:1 – May 16

19:17 – December 21

22:42 – November 27

## JOHN

1:14 – December 24

1:29 – October 14

2:11 – July 10